Enterprise Search

Martin White

O'REILLY®

Beijing · Cambridge · Farnham · Köln · Sebastopol · Tokyo

Enterprise Search

by Martin White

Published by O'Reilly Media, Inc., 1005 Gravenstein Highway North, Sebastopol, CA 95472.

O'Reilly books may be purchased for educational, business, or sales promotional use. Online editions are also available for most titles (*http://my.safaribooksonline.com*). For more information, contact our corporate/institutional sales department: 800-998-9938 or *corporate@oreilly.com*.

Editors: Simon St. Laurent and Meghan Blanchette	**Proofreader:** Christopher Hearse
Production Editor: Christopher Hearse	**Cover Designer:** Karen Montgomery
	Interior Designer: David Futato
	Illustrator: Kara Ebrahim

December 2012:   First Edition

Revision History for the First Edition:

2012-11-21   First release

See *http://oreilly.com/catalog/errata.csp?isbn=9781449330446* for release details.

ISBN: 978-1-449-33044-6

[LSI]

Table of Contents

Preface. xi

1. Searching the Enterprise. 1
   Every Day Is a Decision Day   1
   Information as a Corporate Asset   2
      The Information Paradox   4
      Enterprise Search   5
      Search and Information Retrieval   6
      Search Is a Dialog   7
      Search Has to Be Managed   7
      Why Search Is Important   9
      Summary   11
      Further Reading   11

2. Enterprise Search Is Difficult. 13
   A Day at the Office   13
      There Are 3,245 Results   14
      There Are 9 Results   14
      There Are 230 Results   15
      There Are 400 Results   15
      There Are 425 Results   15
      There Are 390 Results   15
      You Think It's All the Relevant Information   16
   A Short History of Search   16
   A Short History of Information Retrieval   17
   Recall, Precision, and Relevance   18
   Why Can't Our Search Be Like Google?   19
   With Web Search You Have Options   20
   Information Quality   21
      Poor Titles   21

No Author Information 21
Metadata 22
Ambiguous Date Formats 22
Document Structure 22
Language 22
Summary 23
Further Reading 23

3. Defining User Requirements. **25**
Information Seeking Models 26
Another Search Engine! Why? 27
User Requirements and User Satisfaction 27
Climate Surveys 28
Diaries 28
Focus Groups 28
Help Desk Calls 29
Microsoft Product Description Cards 29
Personas 30
Team Meetings 32
Usability Tests 33
Use Cases 33
Analysis 34
Compliance 34
Expertise 34
Induction 34
Item 34
Learning 35
Mobile 35
Monitor 35
Product 35
Task 35
User Interviews 36
User Surveys 37
Search Benchmarking 38
Search Logs 38
Stories 39
User Feedback 39
Writing the User Requirements Report 39
Summary 40
Further Reading 40

4. Planning for Search. **41**

Making a Business Case   42
Invest in Skills Before Software   42
Search Support Team   43
Stakeholder Analysis   44
Business Impact   45
Search Owner   46
Content   47
   Owner   47
   Scope   47
   Document Size and File Formats   47
   Metadata Management   48
   Language   48
   Security   48
Technology   48
Infrastructure   49
Disaster Recovery   49
Security   50
Performance   50
Metadata and Taxonomies   51
Help Desk   52
Usability   52
Training and Support   52
Risks   52
Web Site Search   53
Summary   53
Further reading   53

5. Search Technology Part 1.   55
Content Gathering   56
Connectors   56
Document Filters and Language Identification   57
Parsing and Tokenising   58
Stop Words   59
Stemming and Lemmatization   59
Dates   60
Phrases   60
Processing Pipeline   61
Building and Managing the Index   61
Security and ACLs   63
Query Management   64
Spell Checking   65
Retrieval Models   66

Ranking 67
Summarization 67
Document Thumbnails 68
Summary 68
Further Reading 68

6. Search Technology Part 2. .... **69**
Entity Extraction 69
People Search 71
Federated Search 73
Duplicate and Similar Documents 74
Mobile Search 74
Faceted Search 75
Multilingual Search 77
Search-Based Applications 77
Semantic Search 78
Social Search 78
Text Mining and Sentiment Analysis 79
Summary 79
Further Reading 79

7. The Business of Search. **81**
Industry Structure 82
   Dassault 82
   HP 82
   IBM 82
   Lexmark 82
   Oracle 83
Independent Search Vendors 83
Open Source Search Software 84
Google and Search Appliances 85
Microsoft SharePoint 86
Specialized Search Components 88
Cloud-Based Search 88
OEM Applications 89
Systems Integrators 89
e-Discovery 90
Summary 91
Further Reading 91

8. Specification and Selection. **93**
The Project Teams 94

Specification Project Team   95
Selection Project Team   95
Installation Project Team   95
Project Programme Office   95
The Global Dimension   95
Risk Management   96
Project Schedule   97
Writing the Specification   98
The Story So Far   98
Content Scope   99
User Expectations   99
Information Systems Architecture   99
IT Partnerships   99
Internal Development and Support Resources   99
Security and Identity Management   100
Federated Search Requirements   100
People Databases   100
Project Timetable   100
Functional Specification   100
Connectors and APIs   101
Federated Search User Interfaces   101
Index Freshness   101
Filters and Facets   102
Taxonomy and Metadata Management   102
Search and System Logs   102
Entity Extraction   102
Questions for the Vendors   102
Risk Assessment   102
Project Schedule   103
Project Management Methodology   103
Upgrade Release Schedule   103
Supporting a Global Implementation   103
User Groups   104
Key Employee Strategy   104
License and Support Costs   104
Reference Sites   104
Training   104
Building the Vendor Short List   105
Using a Consultant   106
Using a Implementation Partner   106
Open Source Software Procurement   108
The Best of Both Worlds?   109

	Proof of Concept	109
	Contract Negotiation	110
	Summary	111
	Further Reading	111
9.	**Installation and Implementation.**	**113**
	Project Management	113
	Customer Responsibilities	114
	Implementation Schedule	114
	Knowledge Transfer	115
	The Show Stoppers	116
	Get Indexing!	117
	User Interface Design	117
	Usability and Accessibility Testing	117
	Disaster Recovery Tests	117
	Help Desk	118
	Metadata Management	118
	Communications Plan	118
	Summary	119
	Further Reading	119
10.	**Managing Search.**	**121**
	Search Support Team Roles	121
	Search Manager	122
	Search Technology Manager	122
	Search Analytics Manager	123
	Search Information Specialist	123
	Search User Support Manager	124
	Supporting Global Enterprise Search	125
	Creating a Centre of Search Excellence	126
	Search Team Skills	127
	Introduction to Information Retrieval	127
	Indexing	127
	Retrieval and Ranking	128
	User Interaction and Interface Design	128
	Evaluation of IR Systems	128
	Web Search	128
	Enterprise Search	128
	Help Desk Management	129
	Security and Compliance	130
	Search Liaison Specialists	132
	Reporting Lines	132

Test Searches   133
Best Bets   134
Usability Tests   134
Search Logs   135
    Top 50 Searches by Search Terms/Query   136
    Top 50 Searches Leading to Only a Few or No Results Being Presented   136
    Top 50 Searches Leading to No Document Being Selected   136
    Top 50 Most Requested Documents   136
    Top 50 Searches Where More Than Three Pages of Results Were Presented   137
    Clicks on Best Bets   137
    Clicks on Facets and Filters   137
Feedback Forms   137
Training and Support   137
Establishing Good Communications   138
Summary   138
Further Reading   138

11. A Future for Search. 139
1. The Petabyte Challenge   139
2. Industry Consolidation and Expansion   140
3. The Impact of Microsoft SharePoint   140
4. Big Data and Text Analytics   141
5. Business Intelligence and Unified Information Access   142
6. Mobile Search   143
7. Cross-Session Search   143
8. Social Search   144
9. Federated Search   144
10. Developments in Information Retrieval   145
11. Enterprise Search Professionals   147
12. The Digital Workplace   148
13. Does 'enterprise search' Have a Future?   149
Further Reading   149

12. Critical Success Factors. 151

A. Resources. 153

B. Vendor List. 159

Glossary. 163

Preface

As you walk up Walton Street from the centre of Oxford the road bears slightly to the left and a large 19th century building comes into view. It is not an Oxford college but the headquarters of the Oxford University Press. OUP is the largest university press in the world, and can date its origins back to around 1480. In 1983 I arrived at this building carrying a Texas Silent 700 terminal. This used thermal ink printer technology and had two rubber ears on the top into which a telephone handset could be inserted to link the printer into the BT public telephone network through an acoustic coupler. A decade earlier I had used the same technology to use the first computer-based search services developed by the Lockheed Corporation and System Development Corporation.

I was heading up early attempts by Reed Publishing to develop electronically published products and services, notably airline flight timetables. Reed owned International Computaprint Corporation, based in Fort Washington, PA, which specialized in keyboarding and printing telephone directories and airline timetables. Reed had been working with IBM and the University of Waterloo, Canada on the New Oxford English Dictionary (NOED) project, which was to create a digital version of the Oxford English Dictionary. The OED seeks not only to provide a definitive definition of a word, but also the origins of when the word was first used, with examples of subsequent use which may have modified the definition. All these examples were contained on around 4 million slips of paper.

The proof of concept was to digitize the one of the Supplements to the First Edition, starting at the letter S. The digitization and indexing had now been completed and I, together with Hans Nickel, the founder and CEO of ICC, were about to demonstrate what we had achieved to the NOED project team led by Tim Benbow and Edmund Weiner. Many of the lexicographers were skeptical of the value of the project, and there was a mixture of expectation and disinterest around the table.

With the terminal we set up a connection (at 300 baud!) to the computer in Fort Washington. I can still remember the first question, which came from one of the more skeptical lexicographers, who wanted to know how many words in the OED originated in the Times newspaper. Because all the text had been marked up in Standard Generalized MarkUp (SGML) language (a forerunner of XML) we could identify the source, and not only provide a count but print out (albeit very slowly) all the examples. There was a short period of silence and then these distinguished scholars suddenly realized the potential of information retrieval. They also recognised that it was not going to put them out of a job but enable them to improve the value of the product. Many more queries were undertaken and the session only came to an end when we ran out of supplies of thermal paper.

The NOED project was a great success, not only for the OUP but also for Dr Gaston Gonnet and his team at University of Waterloo. This team became the nucleus of Open Text Corporation. IBM used the knowledge gained from the project in the development of its search technology as the OED files provided a rich source of syntax information to help with query development.

For me it was a day of discovery about the power of search to discover new relationships between items of information. I learned three important lessons from this project. The first of these was the value of metadata structure in searching. Because of the way that the individual elements of the entries had been marked up in SGML it was easy to search for words that had first been used by Charles Dickens after his return from his first visit to the United States in 1842. The second lesson was gained in listening to the members of the project team from IBM and the University of Waterloo as they talked about the importance of computers being able to understand the structure of sentences, work that would lead to the development of semantic search technologies. The third lesson was in understanding the impact that search could have on organizational processes and outputs.

Almost three decades on from that visit to Oxford I am still fascinated and frustrated by the technology of search and the process of searching. In many respects we have not come all that far from the technology I was using in 1974. Google's PageRank is not far removed from Dr. Gene Garfield's development of citation indexes in 1960 and the concepts of recall and precision emerged from research carried out by Cyril Cleverdon at the Cranfield Institute of Technology, UK, in the mid-1960s. The mathematics of vector-space indexing was developed by Dr. Gerald Salton at Cornell University.in 1975 and Dr. Michael Lynch founded Autonomy Ltd. in 1996.

Enterprise search is now moving from a 'nice to have' to a 'need to have' application as organizations struggle to find the information they need to make good business decisions. Not only is more information being created but nothing is being thrown away. Search technology is a mixture of the mathematical management of probability and computational linguistics but this book is not about technology. It is about meeting the expectations of users by investing the skills and experience needed to manage the technology. Whether you are a business manager, IT manager or information professional I hope that when you finish this book you will set up a meeting with your HR Manager and start the process of staffing up your search support team before any further investment in technology.

As you read this book I hope you find what you are looking for

How to Use This Book

This book has been written to help business managers, and the IT teams supporting them, understand why effective enterprise-wide search is essential in any organization, and how to go about the process of meeting user requirements. This could be by improving the existing search application(s) or by specifying and implementing a new search application. Search technology is not easy to understand without a good background in applied mathematics or information science. This book has just two chapters out of twelve on search technology, with the objective of providing just enough detail to understand the possibilities offered by enterprise search and the software available on commercial and open-source terms.

A good place to start might be Chapter 12 on critical success factors. If you are not able to meet at least eight of the twelve success factors then you really do need to read this book.

Chapter 1 and Chapter 2 set the scene, explaining why effective enterprise search is essential to any organization. Over the last couple of years a number of surveys have been published which show that most organizations are finding it increasingly difficult to find information that has been created at some considerable cost in terms of staff time. It is not just that the volume of information being created as increased but that low storage costs mean that nothing is now thrown away. The user research techniques described in Chapter 3 may well come up with some uncomfortable outcomes as you may find that your colleagues are reduced to emailing around the organization to find the information they need to make business-critical decisions. Chapter 4 considers the elements of an enterprise search strategy, highlighting the importance of allocating an adequate level of staffing to the support of search. An organization with more than 1000 employees probably needs a search support team of two people, and above around 10,000 employees this will double.

Chapter 5 and Chapter 6 provide an outline of the technology of search. The search functionality described in Chapter 5 is the base-level technology that can be delivered by virtually all search applications and then Chapter 6 offers an overview of functionality that will often mark out differences between various search software options. The search business is not a large one. There are perhaps no more than 100 vendors globally and the structure of the industry and the challenges it faces are discussed in Chapter 7.

If the result of the user research and business planning is that a new search application is required then Chapter 8 and Chapter 9 cover the process of defining the business and search requirements, the evaluation of commercial and open-source software and the management of the installation and implementation.

If you only have time to read one chapter please read Chapter 10. The reason for the well-documented lack of satisfaction with a search application is that organizations invest in technology but not staff with the expertise and experience to gain the best possible return on the investment through reviewing search logs and monitoring changes in user requirements. Finally Chapter 11 gives an overview of some of the current directions in search development.

There is one topic that is not covered in this book, and that is the design of search user interfaces. This is a very important topic in its own right and many excellent books have been, and are being, written.

The book concludes with a list of books and blogs on information retrieval and enterprise search, lists of search vendors and search integrators and a glossary.

Safari® Books Online

 Safari Books Online (*www.safaribooksonline.com*) is an on-demand digital library that delivers expert content in both book and video form from the world's leading authors in technology and business.

Technology professionals, software developers, web designers, and business and creative professionals use Safari Books Online as their primary resource for research, problem solving, learning, and certification training.

Safari Books Online offers a range of product mixes and pricing programs for organizations, government agencies, and individuals. Subscribers have access to thousands of books, training videos, and prepublication manuscripts in one fully searchable database from publishers like O'Reilly Media, Prentice Hall Professional, Addison-Wesley Professional, Microsoft Press, Sams, Que, Peachpit Press, Focal Press, Cisco Press, John Wiley & Sons, Syngress, Morgan Kaufmann, IBM Redbooks, Packt, Adobe Press, FT Press, Apress, Manning, New Riders, McGraw-Hill, Jones & Bartlett, Course Technology, and dozens more. For more information about Safari Books Online, please visit us online.

How to Contact Us

Please address comments and questions concerning this book to the publisher:

O'Reilly Media, Inc.
1005 Gravenstein Highway North

Sebastopol, CA 95472
800-998-9938 (in the United States or Canada)
707-829-0515 (international or local)
707-829-0104 (fax)

We have a web page for this book, where we list errata, examples, and any additional information. You can access this page at *http://oreil.ly/Enterprise-Search*.

To comment or ask technical questions about this book, send email to *bookques tions@oreilly.com*.

For more information about our books, courses, conferences, and news, see our website at *http://www.oreilly.com*.

Find us on Facebook: *http://facebook.com/oreilly*

Follow us on Twitter: *http://twitter.com/oreillymedia*

Watch us on YouTube: *http://www.youtube.com/oreillymedia*

Acknowledgments

I could not have written this book without the generous support of many colleagues over quite a number of years. In particular my good friend Miles Kehoe (New Idea Engineering) read through every line of the book at quite short notice and made many invaluable comments and suggestions. Over the years I have learned a great deal about the search business and search technology from Miles and his business partner Mark Bennett and it is a great shame that Miles and his team are eight time zones away from Horsham. Despite the diligent work that Miles has undertaken the responsibility for errors and omissions is mine alone.

Stephen Arnold, my co-author for Successful Enterprise Search Management, has been a constant source of insight into the technologies and business of search for over a decade. Charlie Hull (Flax) has patiently educated me about open-source search implementation and Valentin Richter (Raytion) has done the same for the implementation of commercial enterprise search applications.

Information Today Inc. have given me the opportunity to participate in the Enterprise Search Summit and Enterprise Search Summit Fall conferences in the USA and supported my ambition to establish Enterprise Search Europe in 2011. Also at Information Today Michelle Manafy and then Theresa Cramer allowed me to voice my opinions on search in a long-running Eureka column in e-Content Magazine.

In 2011 the Institute for Prospective Technological Studies, Joint Research Centre, European Commission awarded me a contract to undertake a techno-economic study of the enterprise search market in the EU. The research undertaken during the project has been of great value in writing this book and I am grateful to Dr Stavri Nikolov, the IPTS project manager, for his support and insight throughout the project.

Tony Byrne (Real Story Group) has been a constant support to me for over a decade in helping me understand search from both a vendor and user perspective, and generously allowed me to use the RSG enterprise search glossary as the basis for the glossary in this book.

Other colleagues whose contributions in various ways have shaped my understanding of search technology and search good practice include Denise Bedford, Jed Cawthorne, Paul Clough, Mike Davis, Susan Farrell, Susan Feldman, David Hawking, John E. Hall, Cathy Hein, Jane McConnell, Elizabeth Marsh, Kristian Norling, Howard McQueen, Peter Morville, Lynda Moulton, Matt Mullen, Mike O'Donoghue, Leslie Owen, Alan Pelz-Sharpe, Avi Rappoport, James Robertson, Lou Rosenfeld and Mark Vadgama. Helen Carley at Facet Publishing and Steve Newton at Galatea were the publishers of two previous books on search. Dr. David James and his colleagues at the Royal Society of Chemistry have been a pleasure to work my role as Chair of the RSC e-Content Committee.

Janus Boye (JBoye), Kurt Kragh Sørensen (IntraTeam), Jakob Nielsen (Nielsen Norman Group) and Erik Hartman have given me many opportunities to run search workshops at their events, and these have been an invaluable opportunity to learn from the experiences of enterprise search managers.

Over the last decade I have carried out many enterprise search consulting assignments but I am not in a position to list the organizations involved. Each of these assignments has given me additional insights into the technology and use of enterprise search.

I would like to thank Simon St. Laurent and Meghan Blanchette at O'Reilly Media for their support in bringing this book from an initial idea to a published book in just ten months. It is a privilege to be an O'Reilly author. In my book Intranet Management Handbook, published in 2011, I announced that I would not be writing any more books. This is an e-book. It doesn't count!

It has not been easy for my wife Cynthia when people ask her what I do for a living. Being an information scientist is fascinating for me but difficult for Cynthia to describe. She has been immensely supportive during eleven career changes and eight books. Our son Simon manages my IT requirements including the design and support of the Intranet Focus web site and I must mention his wife Andrea.

During the course of this book our first grandchild was born to Nick and Andrea. (We have two Andreas and two Dr. Whites in our family!) Noah had a very difficult start to his life but is now progressing very well. This book is dedicated to him so that when he begins his career in a very digital world he can say that it was his grandfather who wrote the first e-book on enterprise search. You will come across his name again in this book.

—Martin White
Horsham, UK, October 2012

CHAPTER 1

Searching the Enterprise

It seemed like a normal day when you arrived at work and turned on your computer. Then, the phone rang. Colleagues of yours were just about to go into a meeting with a prospective customer, and they needed details about custom software they had proposed installing. You went to search for those details, and they weren't in the standard specification sheet, nor were they in the release notes, nor were they in any of the first fifty results your company's search tool produced.

Every Day Is a Decision Day

We have to make many decisions every day. Each of those decisions required enough information to make the decision as risk-free as possible. In many cases, though, we probably did not have the time needed to find all the relevant information. We probably prided ourselves on being good enough managers not to need information; our experience enabled us to make the decision!

Every day, however, people make the news headlines because they made the wrong decision. The financial meltdown on 2008 was arguably an information problem. Loans had been made to people purchasing homes without adequate security. The pressures of making sales targets led to an inadequate review of the circumstances of the people asking for loans and senior managers in the banks had no information about the scale of the problem. While your decisions may not result in you making the news, a failure to make the best decision possible on the basis of the best available information could be bad news for your career.

Once upon a time you could at least walk into your office in the morning and feel reasonably certain about the decisions you would need to make. With the arrival of 24/7 mobile access, reductions in staff, and difficult economic and market conditions you may well get a call at any time during the day from a colleagues just about to walk into a sales opportunity who have just realized that they did not have a critical piece of information about the client or the proposal they were making.

That puts the pressure on to find information that could have a very positive impact on the bottom line. Fortunately your company has invested in an enterprise search application, so you enter a few keywords into the search box, sit back and within a few seconds you discover that the company either seems to have no information at all on the query you have made, or you find that there are over 3000 items of information and you only have a few minutes to provide a response to your colleague.

When we are dealing with decisions that are based on some standard business processes, such as setting up a project or writing a monthly report, then we often rely on browsing through the information architecture of an intranet, shared file collection or a document management system to find the information we need.

Search becomes critical when there is time pressure and a need for an immediate solution. We expect it to be as easy to use as Google and at least as effective, providing us with the information we need on the first page of results. Anything less, and the search application is regarded as a failure. Google or Bing have huge scale and an immense amount of development has gone in to providing search experiences across the Web. Searching for information inside a single company seems like it should be easier, but often isn't.

This book will provide you with enough information to understand how enterprise search works, to help you in the decision of choosing the right solution for your company, and then getting the best return on the investment in the technology and the people who are responsible for making sure search works.

Information as a Corporate Asset

Many companies attach asset numbers to all of their property, be it a wastepaper bin or a complex machine tool. All those assets are logged in a database and their residual financial value will be given on the balance sheet of the company. The balance sheet will also show the financial assets of the business.

No matter how hard you look there will be two corporate assets missing from the balance sheet. One of these is the employees, though at least there will be a record in the Annual Report, of how many employees there are, possibly categorized by location or gender. But what about the information assets of the business, and the knowledge assets possessed by each employee no matter what their age or grade? International accounting standards do not allow for information to be capitalized as an asset because there is no definitive way of calculating its value. The value of a piece of information is unique to an individual at a particular point in time. In search terms it has a different 'relevance' and there is much more to say about relevance later in this book.

Not only is every physical asset recorded by the company, but someone will own the asset and make a decision about when and how it should be replaced or upgraded. In most companies no-one owns information as a corporate asset, even though there may be someone with the title of Chief Information Officer. There is now a growing concern by senior managers about the sheer scale of corporate information resources with the arrival of the concept of Big Data. With hundreds of applications being used each day inside even a modest-sized company the amount of data and information that is being collected is often poorly understood. Worse, because of the low cost of storage nothing is every deleted, so the rate of growth is a combination of new information and old information, with the assumption that all information has a value. It may do if it can be found!

The term 'unstructured information' is widely used to describe documents, emails, blogs and other text information, and more recently to rich media applications. In fact this information does have a structure, in that there is usually a title, an author, a date, and perhaps section headings and tables. The term came into use to distinguish these categories of information from 'structured' databases where data is stored in defined fields such as Address Line1, Address Line 2, Town etc. For many years the UK search vendor Autonomy made much of the fact that unstructured information represented 80% of the total information assets of the organization. No evidence was ever presented for this assertion, which seemed to be based solely on the Pareto principle. More important there is no relationship between volume and value.

Until recently enterprise search was used primarily to search unstructured text and so had to be able to cope with the issues of language and semantics.

Take these two sentences:

Noah loaded boxes into the van.
Noah loaded the van with boxes.

In the case of the first sentence the number of boxes could be any number of two upwards. In the second sentence there is the implicit message that the van was totally full of boxes, though we cannot be sure.

The textual differences between the sentences are very small but semantically very important. In almost every conversation we have we are constantly checking whether we have fully understood what others are saying, perhaps asking for clarification from time to time. In the case of a document that might have been written several years ago we cannot have this type of conversation, and yet we expect a search engine to be able to read and understand the document, and then be able to say with certainty that the document contains information that is relevant to the search we have carried out and list it in the top few results.

The Information Paradox

One of the outcomes of the Big Data movement is that at last there are some metrics for the scale of corporate data and information resources. Over the last couple of years that research has started to be undertaken into the way in which corporate information is being managed and the level of investment in enterprise search. These surveys have been carried out by MarkLogic, Symantec, Smartlogic, Findwise, AIIM, and Oracle.

Quotes from some of these studies include:

> In a global survey of 1,375 subscribers conducted in January 2010, 85% of respondents said that information is a key strategic asset, yet only 36% said their organizations are currently well positioned to use information to help grow their business. The disparity at the upper end of the scale was even more dramatic; while almost half—45%—strongly agreed that information is a key strategic asset, only 7% believed they are very well positioned to exploit it. This research study overall makes it clear that making the transition to an information-based economy is not easy. Executives know information is a key strategic asset, that managing it well will provide real value and competitive advantage, but they are not sure how to do that, and there is a certain ambivalence about the role of IT.
>
> —Harvard Business Review Analytic Services

> 40% of respondents say that management at their organizations is either only "slightly" aware or not aware at all of the extent to which unstructured data exists in their enterprises. This lack of management awareness means it may be difficult for data managers to secure the funding and resources needed to properly secure, store, and fully leverage the large volumes of unstructured data coming into their organizations.
>
> —MarkLogic (2011)

> A majority of respondents report that unstructured data is an essential part of their business, meaning that it may be a component of services or products offered to customers or constituents. At least 57% indicate that unstructured data plays an "extremely" or "very" important role in their businesses. About one out of five, or 18%, consider unstructured data to be at the core of their business.
>
> —MarkLogic (2011)

> Enterprise search is falling far short of expectations, according to a survey of more than 2,000 directors and managers in the US, UK, Germany and France. More than half (52%) of respondents say they cannot find the information they are seeking using their own

organization's enterprise search facility within what most define as an acceptable amount of time. Nearly two-thirds of those surveyed (65%) define a 'good search' as taking less than two minutes to find what they were looking for, but only 48% report being able to achieve that result in their own organization.

—Smartlogic (2011)

The Enterprise Search and Findability survey has shown that the majority of the respondents find it difficult to find relevant information within the organization. To be more precise, 60% of the respondents expressed that it is very/moderately hard to find the right information. Only 11% stated that it is fairly easy to search for information and as few as 3% consider it very easy to find the desirable information. The ease of finding the right information clearly has a connection with the size of the organization. When looking at organizations with less than 1000 employees, one can see that 31% of the respondents feel that it is moderately/very hard to find the right information, while the corresponding percentage for organizations with 1001 or more employees is 77%. Nearly half of the respondents (44%) were mostly or very dissatisfied with their search application.

—Findwise (2012)

93% of executives believe their organization is losing revenue as a result of not being able to fully leverage the information they collect. On average, they estimate this lost opportunity to be 14% of annual revenue.

—Oracle (2012)

Overall the view is that information is becoming more important, more difficult to find, and no one wants to take a lead position in improving the situation.

Before you read on, where would you place your organization in the spectrum of being adequately prepared for information abundance? Knowing the scale of the problem is the first step in finding a solution.

Enterprise Search

It is time for some definitions. This book is entitled *Enterprise Search* so what is 'enterprise search'? Here's one possible definition:

An enterprise search application enables employees to find all the information that the company possesses without the need to know where the information is stored.

The position I take in this book is that enterprise search is not about selecting and installing a single search application that will index every item of information and data owned by the organization.

In my view enterprise search is about creating a managed search environment that enables employees to find the information they need to achieve organizational and/or personal objectives. It should also include site search for corporate web sites. It should also include site search for corporate web sites.

Many companies already have one or more search application, either operating as a discrete search application or embedded into another enterprise application. Trying to replace all of these with one HAL-like enterprise search application is not a realistic strategy. Replacing some of them might be.

Search and Information Retrieval

Information retrieval can be regarded as the science (largely mathematics) behind search. It is a branch of information science and dates back to the mid 1950s. It has been defined as follows:

Information retrieval deals with the representation, storage, organization of and access to information items such as documents, Web pages, online catalogues, structured and semi-structured records and multimedia objects.

There are two different perspectives of information retrieval research. One perspective considers the computer technology of information retrieval, such as ways of building efficient indexes and finding ways to handle multiple languages. The second perspective is user-based, looking at search user interfaces and how people go about constructing search queries. Although there are some very distinguished university departments of information science around the world (many now called iSchools) few teach information retrieval in any depth as an undergraduate course and this means that the annual output of graduates with skills in search implementation is very low indeed. Computer science departments, of which there are many more, also pay little attention to the science and technology of enterprise search. It should also be noted that many of the major IT vendors, such as IBM, Oracle, HP and Microsoft, have a long history of carrying out information retrieval research, as of course does Google.

The scale of the science behind search can be seen in the fact that the standard textbook on information retrieval by Ricardo Baeza-Yates and Berthier Ribeiro-Neto runs to 760 pages of text and almost 2000 references in the bibliography. The definitive book on the design of search user interfaces by Marti Hearst is over 300 pages in length and has around 500 references in the bibliography to research papers on user interface design.

Sadly there seems to be a gulf between the information retrieval community and the enterprise search community. Some of the information retrieval conferences do have a session where papers from the commercial search world are presented. The situation is now starting to change and in the future much closer ties are likely to develop between the information retrieval community and search software vendors and users.

Search Is a Dialog

Earlier in this chapter I remarked on how in conversations we are constantly engaged in a dialog to ensure that we understand what the people we are talking with are trying to convey. It is very important to understand that search is a dialog. We tend to see search as a 'first strike' application; just putting a search term into Google or Bing provides all that the search application and we need to deliver a page of useful results. The reality is that even on Google we are sometimes prompted on spelling or asked 'did you mean'. On the left hand side of the page there may be filters that we can use to narrow down our search, and on public search sites there will be paid-for advertising that also offers solutions to our problems.

We often go into a large department store to find a birthday present, and yet I have never come across a store with a Birthday Present Department. We may look at the store directory (the information architecture) for ideas, but if we are in a hurry we may also go to the Information Desk (the query box) for advice. There we will be asked the age and gender of the person for whom we are buying a present, and what their interests are, in order to suggest one or more specific departments we might wish to explore. Once in the Sports Goods section we may have another conversation with a floor manager about which is the best set of soccer goalkeeping gloves.

The challenge with search, as is the case for the staff of the Information Desk, is that every user is different, with their own individual perceptions of what would make a good birthday present and what would represent value for money. In the business environment is challenge is to find a way of meeting the individual expectations of each member of staff without having to provide them with their own individual search application. Indeed the aim is to make them think that indeed it does work just the way they want it to. Enterprise search is a constant battle between providing personal power at a price that the company can afford.

Search Has to Be Managed

For over a decade I have been providing consulting services in management of intranets, and one of the most common issues is who should be taking responsibility for intranet development and operation in a company. An intranet, like search, is a very high touch application, with most if not all employees using the intranet every day. The information on an intranet will be authored by most departments in the company but clearly the people managing the application need to report to a manager who has the budget to support the intranet. The end result is that intranet can be owned by Corporate Communications, HR, IT, or even Marketing on the basis that an intranet is just another web site.

In the final analysis it should not matter who owns search, and the same situation applies to an intranet. Both should be managed within an overall information management policy and an information management strategy, but very rarely are. Some years ago I went to run an intranet workshop for a major UK organization for which the effective management of information was probably its main competitive advantage. When I arrived I noticed that all the cars were reverse parked, and it looked very neat and tidy. It transpired that the organization was concerned about safety and at the end of the day did not want staff reversing out of a parking space and either crashing into another car or staff walking to their cars. The parking policy was published on the intranet and at the reception desk and it was made clear that a very dim view would be taken if the policy was not followed.

However this organization did not have any policies about the management of information, so almost every document was written in a different format, often with no owner or even a date on the document. The quality of the search experience is directly related to the quality of the content. The old adage of Garbage In – Garbage Out applies to search more than any other application. Someone has to take responsibility for information quality within an overall information management strategy. This is ideally written around an information life-cycle, of which the following is just one example. The use of the term 'document' is just a convenience and could be any item of information from a personal profile to a video file. The following is an example of an information life-cycle:

1. *Create*

    This is the process of creating documents in a way that enables the document to progress through the stages of the information lifecycle. These might include document categories, writing good titles and adding metadata. There could also be a quality assurance process.

2. *Store*

    There are many places that documents could be stored. These might include local and shared drives, document management applications, Lotus Notes applications and intranets. A set of criteria needs to be established so that employees know where documents should be stored so that they can be located and accessed by any employee with permission to do so.

3. *Discover*

    Information can be found by searching through repositories, browsing through folder structures and intranet navigation and through alerting services such as wikis and blogs. Each has a role to play in the discovery process. The process can be facilitated by good usability and the design of intuitive lists.

4. *Use*

    Documents can be used only subject to rules on confidentiality, security and personal privacy. These rules and guidelines need to be established.

5. Share

To be of benefit to an organisation documents have to be able to be shared internally, with third parties and with the public. Users of these document have to be confident that the information they contain can be trusted to be reliable, and that if needed the documents are available in a number of different languages.

6. Review

As documents are shared others may have views on the accuracy and value of the document. Processes need to be agreed for undertaking the review process and if needed creating a new version of the document. A possible decision could be that the document is disposed of to prevent inadvertent use at some time in the future.

7. Record

Some documents will need to be retained in a secure environment for an agreed period of time. Details of retention periods need to be agreed which take into account legal and regulatory requirements, and product and service lifetimes.

8. Dispose

Disposal is the final stage of the information lifecycle and it is the point the document has no further value to the company and can be deleted from all systems without any risk to the future integrity of the company.

Why Search Is Important

The biggest single challenge that any search manager faces is making a business case for a level of investment in search that is appropriate to the requirements of the company. Although the process of making a business case is covered in Chapter 7 let me end this chapter with seven of the main business benefits of good enterprise search.

Capitalizing on information investment

Every day most employees will have spent time on creating information; everything from writing a business plan, sending an email or reporting on a visit to a customer. The process of creation may well be of the order of an hour a day, or 12% of the working year. If this information cannot be found and used by other employees then that time has been wasted twice over, as other employees may have had to create the information all over again. There is also information from external sources, such as market research reports, that has been purchased and will have a company-wide value beyond the original purchaser.

Without enterprise search how much time and effort will be wasted? The outcomes of the 2012 Oracle study quoted above were that 93% of executives believe their organization is losing revenue as a result of not being able to fully leverage the information they collect. On average, they estimate this lost opportunity to be 14% of annual revenue.

Reactive to business opportunities

At a time when business growth is static finding new business opportunities is of the highest importance. When an opportunity does arise the speed with which the company can find examples of relevant experience or size the market potential could make all the difference between winning the business and being a poor second.

If a business opportunity arrived on your desk today how quickly could you respond with a proposal that had low risk and a good financial margin? An enterprise search application could reduce the research time from days to hours, if not minutes.

Making the best use of staff expertise

It is important not to focus just on information but also on knowledge. Knowledge cannot be written down as it is context-specific and changes day-by-day as new knowledge is gained. Typically companies have employee turnover rates of 10% a year. In a company with 5000 employees that means that on average every working day two people arrive at the company to build their careers and enable the company to meet its objectives. How do employees find out who knows what

How certain can you be that you know every employee that has expertise that would be of value to you? Enterprise search can play a major role in finding them.

Bringing new staff on board more quickly

New employees want to make a positive contribution as quickly as possible. They do not have the time or the inclination to work through the navigation of the intranet or the folder structure in the document management system, nor do they know the names of people that might be useful to them as they begin work.

Employees taking on new roles and responsibilities will be in just the same position, but possibly with a greater need to get up to speed as the expectation will be that they know exactly where all the relevant information will be located. If only!

Speeding the process of acquisition

One of the most significant benefits of enterprise search is that once the deal has been done employees in the acquired company need to have immediate access to the information resources and employee knowledgebase of their new employer. In addition business case for the acquisition will have been based on the skills and knowledge that the acquired business will bring.

In those crucial early days enterprise search can make a substantial contribution to the rapid and successful integration of the acquired company by quickly indexing the information resources of the acquired company.

Supporting mobile workers

Many of these employees will be working outside of the office, dealing with customers, prospects and suppliers. They will need information as the meeting is taking place to confirm the details of a product or the name of a subject-matter expert in the company.

Mobile users will use enterprise search on their smartphone or tablet to find information on a close-to-instantaneous basis and close the deal.

Reducing workplace stress

Routine tasks are rarely routine. New policies emerge and new forms are devised to capture information. Of course what is a routine task for a long-serving employee is not routine for someone new to the company or the role. In both cases there never seems to be enough time to complete the tasks.

Embedding search into a task can ensure that as the task is undertaken the most recent information is presented to the employee by the enterprise search application working in the background as a search-based application.

Summary

All the evidence suggests that organizations are ill-prepared for the rate of growth of information they are experiencing. Because information is not seen as an information asset, with an associated information management strategy, organizations have no view on the scale of the problem. As a result no one is taking ownership of the problem because 'there is no problem'. According to a survey carried out by Oracle the result is that there could be a 14% loss of revenues for the corporate sector. Seeing 'enterprise search' as the quest for a single search application that can index all organizational information is not the solution. Enterprise search is about creating a managed search environment that enables employees to find the information they need to achieve organizational and/or personal objectives. There will be many different business cases that need to be addressed within this managed search environment, each contributing to the overall investment case.

Further Reading

A list of books and blogs can be found in Appendix A at the end of this book with a section pertinent to this chapter in the "Further Reading" (page 156) section.

CHAPTER 2

Enterprise Search Is Difficult

Most people think that search is easy. All you have to do is type a word or two into the query box on Google or Bing. In a fraction of a second, thousands, if not millions, of results are ready to review. You don't know and don't care about how this was accomplished, and for searching the Internet that's acceptable. Even if you knew all about PageRank, BigTable, Markov chains and the teleportation matrix it would be of no value in using Google and the situation is similar with Bing. The nice thing about searching the web is that we are easily satisfied. Even if you don't find quite what you are looking for you will find something close enough to be useful and forget about the initial disappointment.

Enterprise search is much more challenging. From the evidence presented in Chapter 1 it is clear that there is a significant dissatisfaction with enterprise search applications. One of the reasons for this is that the height of the satisfaction barrier. If you are looking for a specific document or specific information and cannot find it then your satisfaction is zero. Finding something roughly similiar is rarely good enough to risk your career on.

When it comes to enterprise search it really does make a lot of sense to know something about how search works. However before we start to look inside the boxes in Chapter 5 and Chapter 6 in this chapter we will look at some typical experiences with enterprise search and then in Chapter 3 consider some ways in which we can define the search requirements of our employees.

A Day at the Office

Over the first coffee of the day you've been looking through the overnight emails, and found one from your manager asking you to prepare the section on corporate social responsibility for the Annual Report. As your company has acquired Advanced Energy Corporation and Building Benchmark Services in the course of the last 12 months your manager has suggested it would be a good idea to check out what their approach has been to corporate social responsibility in case there are lessons to be learned.

As this is the first time you have been asked to write this section your initial action is to see what can be found on Google just to make sure you know exactly what corporate social responsibility is all about. In just over 0.2 seconds Google comes back with over 10 million results. Impressive! The first result is from Wikipedia listing all the various different terms used for corporate social responsibility.

Next you turn to the search box and enter 'corporate social responsibility'. The initial response is to ask you whether you want to search the intranet, the document management system, or all sources. Your immediate reaction is to wonder why you have to know where information is before you search for it, and then to wonder why anyone would choose to search in a specific application rather than all the applications that the company has invested in.

For now you decide to search in all the applications. After perhaps 15-20 seconds (much slower than Google when it was searching the world!) you get some results back and are faced with one or more of the following scenarios.

There Are 3,245 Results

Your first reaction will be that you do not have the time to look through 3,245 results but that will not be a problem as all the relevant results will be on the first couple of pages. However as you look through the initial set of results the titles are often meaningless, such as Doc1 or 6635RTS. Looking at the summaries of the results you then realise that the words 'corporate', 'social' and 'responsibility' are highlighted but in many cases not as a phrase, and it dawns on you that you have been presented with results that contain any of the three words and not just about 'corporate social responsibility'.

There Are 9 Results

Surely there must be more than nine results? Where are the rest of them? Then you think back to the Wikipedia entry and remember that 'corporate social responsibility' is often shorted to the acronym CSR and none of the results show any reference to CSR. Now you are faced with the problem of how to search for documents that contain either the phrase 'corporate social responsibility' or 'CSR'. This is starting to be more difficult than you imagined. You move to the Advanced Search option and start again

There Are 230 Results

The problem is that many seem to be about construction regulations. This is when you realize that CSR also stands for Construction Safety Register, which is an important for the Construction Division of your company but has no relationship at all to corporate social responsibility. You have no idea how to include only references to CSR for Corporate Social Responsbility when searching for CSR.

There Are 400 Results

However, most of these results have different versions of the same document. Preparing the official Corporate Social Responsibility document usually means going through many versions before the final document is approved. Because you are searching the document management application as well as the intranet all these versions are now visible and it is impossible to tell which the final versions from the interim versions.

There Are 425 Results

None of them seem to be previous Corporate Social Responsibility reports. What has happened is that the Report has been added to the company's web site but no one has been tasked with putting it up on the intranet as there is a link on the intranet to the corporate web site in case anyone wants to look at it. Of course everyone knows this but the search application does not.

There Are 390 Results

But none of these results seem to be from Advanced Energy Corporation and very few are from Building Benchmark Services. Looking in more detail at the results which have BBS somewhere in the URL you see that 'corporate' has been highlighted but the adjacent word is 'citizenship' and you begin to realize that BBS have a section in their Annual Report headed Corporate Citizenship rather than Corporate Social Responsibility. Now you have to think about how to create a new search query to bring in the concept of citizenship. As for Advanced Energy it is probable that for some reason the search application is not indexing the Advanced Energy application that contains the work the company undertook on corporate social responsibility. Now you will have to track down who was responsible for this activity, hoping that they are still employed by your company.

You Think It's All the Relevant Information

It has been a good day. The search application gave you twenty really useful documents from the 83 it listed out, including the statements from Advanced Energy Corporation and BBS. You spend the rest of the day writing up a statement about your company's approach to corporate social responsibility and email it to your manager. You take an early train home.

On the journey your manager calls you and wants to know why the outcomes of the project on CSR that the Project Prospero team have been working on for the last few months is not included in your analysis. You promise to check and log on to the corporate desktop through your iPad. Re-running the search fails to disclose anything about a report from Project Prospero, and indeed there is nothing about Project Prospero.

The next morning you call a friend in the Project Management Office and through her track down Simon, the project manager. That is when you discover that he and a group from legal have been working on CSR issues using a TeamSite in SharePoint 2010. This can only be accessed by people that are part of the group, and as the search application knew that you were not a member it did not show you documents from the TeamSite. Simon is more than willing to add you to the TeamSite, and your manager accepts your explanation.

But you resolve not to put your trust in the search application again. Ever!

These are just illustrative of the typical problems that arise with enterprise search. Managing them requires a combination of high quality content, search technology selected with care, and a team of people supporting the technology and users.

A Short History of Search

Search came into prominence with the advent of the web search services in the 1990s, notably Alta Vista, Google, Microsoft and Yahoo. However the history of search technology goes back much further than this. Arguably the story starts with Douglas Engelbart, a remarkable electrical engineer whose main claim to fame is that he invented the mouse that is now a standard control device for personal computers. In 1959 Engelbart started up the Augmented Human Intellect program at the Stanford Research Institute in Menlo Park, California. One of his research students was Charles Bourne, who worked on whether it would be possible to transform the batch search retrieval technology developed in the 1950s into a service based on a large mainframe computer which users could connect to over a network.

By 1963 SRI was able to demonstrate the first 'online' information retrieval service using a cathode ray tube (CRT) device to interact with the computer. It is worth remembering that the computers being used for this service had 64K of core memory. Even at this early stage of development the facility to cope with spelling variants was implemented in the software. Other pioneers included System Development Corporation, Massachusetts Institute of Technology and Lockheed. The main focus of these online systems was to provide researchers with access to large files of abstracts of scientific literature to support research into space technology and other large scale scientific and engineering projects.

It should not be thought that all the developments were taking place in the USA. In the UK a team at the United Kingdom Atomic Energy Authority took the lead in using mini-computers to support online services.

These services were only able to search short text documents, such as abstracts of scientific papers. In the late 1960s two new areas of opportunity arose which prompted work into how to search the full text of documents. One was to support the work of lawyers who needed to search through case reports to find precedents. The second was also connected to the legal profession, and arose from the US Department of Justice deciding to break up what it regarded as monopolies in the computer industry (targeting IBM) and later the telecommunications industry, where AT&T was the target. These actions led IBM in particular to make a massive investment into full-text search which by 1969 led to the development of STAIRS (Storage and Information Retrieval System) which was subsequently released as a commercial IBM application. This was the first enterprise search application and remained in the IBM product catalogue.

The problem with STAIRS was that at least in its initial versions it could only search for words that appeared in the document. What researchers wanted was to find information about concepts that were not present as words in a document, especially if they were working for the security services. Dynamite can be used for mining but also to make a bomb, and they needed a search system that would present results that included dynamite to a search query on bomb making. One of the innovators in the mid-1980s in developing concept searching was Advanced Decision Systems. Verity was the name of the company that was spun off from ADS to bid (successfully) on a US DOD/US Air Force project. A feature of the Verity Query Language was the capability to weight topics against a taxonomy tree. Verity was also able to offer real-time indexing. Verity became one of the most innovative companies in enterprise search, and in 2003 it acquired the enterprise search business of Inktomi Corp., relaunching the application as Ultraseek. Then in 2005 Verity was acquired by the UK-based search company Autonomy. The story of the enterprise search industry continues in Chapter 6.

A Short History of Information Retrieval

One of the problems facing anyone interested in search is that there are a number of parallel domains:

- Enterprise search
- Site search of a public web site

- Internet search
- Search engine optimization
- Information retrieval

Internet search and search engine optimization fall outside of the scope of this book but information retrieval certainly does not, and yet is probably a totally unfamiliar topic to most search managers.

The term was first used by Calvin Mooers, like Englebart a pioneer in the early history of the development of computer technology in the 1950s and 1960s. Mooers made the point that one of the challenges of information retrieval is that the person contributing the information to a system has no idea of when the information will be found by a searcher and what it will be used for.

In 1959 he coined Mooers Law and its corollary:

> An information retrieval system will tend not to be used whenever it is more painful and troublesome for a customer to have information than for him not to have it.
>
> Where an information retrieval system tends not to be used, a more capable information retrieval system may tend to be used even less.

The second Law needs a brief explanation. What Mooers realised was that if a user has a poor experience with an information retrieval system they are unlikely to try again in another system even if they are told it will produce better results. They are more likely to send an email or call someone on the telephone.

Around the world there are probably several hundred academic departments offering courses in information science, of which information retrieval is a core topic. Information science is one of the sciences behind search in addition to mathematical probability, computational linguistics and computer science. Much of the research in information retrieval is based on well-defined sets of documents and other content items but the problem for enterprise search is that the sets of documents are very ill-defined. The two communities do talk to each other and certainly some of the developments that have taken place in all areas of web search, internet search and enterprise search have come from the information retrieval (often known as IR) community.

Recall, Precision, and Relevance

These three topics in enterprise search are foundation topics in information retrieval. Two seem easy to define:

- Recall is a measure of the number of relevant documents returned as a percentage of all the relevant documents in a collection.

- Precision is a measure of the extent to which the set of documents returned from a search are relevant.

Basis Technology offers a good illustration of these two terms:

> Suppose you are searching for red balls from a box that contains seven red balls and eight green balls. Blindfolded, you pull out eight balls, of which four are red and four are green. Precision is the number of correct items over the total number of items found. That is, you found four red (which you wanted) and pulled out eight balls in total, thus precision is four/eight (half of your results were correct) or 50%.

> Recall asks the question on: "Of all the correct items, how many did I find?" In this case, there were seven correct items (because there are seven red balls) and you found four, thus your recall is four/seven or 57%.

However the problem with both precision and recall is that both are defined in terms of relevance which is a personal judgment on the value of a piece of information. In an ideal world any result from a search should produce a list of all, and only, relevant documents. This is impossible because there is no way of knowing, at least outside of a test collection, how many relevant documents are in a given collection. Another problem is that relevance is defined in absolute terms; either a document is relevant or it is not. In reality things are fuzzy.

Search vendors often talk about 'accurate' results. This is nonsense. Information can be accurate in terms of totally representing a known and agreed fact, for example that Horsham (where I live) is a town in West Sussex. Except that there is a town called Horsham just outside of Philadelphia and another in the state of Victoria, Australia! If a representative from a search vendor tells you that the results from the search software are more accurate than from their competitors always ask them for a definition of accurate and a demonstration!

Why Can't Our Search Be Like Google?

Many companies who are dissatisfied with their current enterprise search application want to know why it is not as good as Google. This is a very good question, and deserves to be answered. The slick answer is that if they allocated around 10,000 engineers to supporting enterprise search in their company then it probably would be as good as Google.

The technology behind the Google internet search is extremely complex and mostly hidden from view. The technology behind Microsoft Bing and other web search sites is equally complex and even more hidden from view.

The story starts in 1997 when Jon Kleinberg, a research scientist at the IBM Almaden Laboratories in Silicon Valley started to look at how the hyperlinks between pages and sites in the World Wide Web could be used to enhance search performance. The algorithms were powerful but as IBM was not in the web search business the outcomes of the research were not of direct value to IBM but were taken up to some extent by Yahoo!

At around the same time Sergey Brin and Larry Page were working on what would become Google. They announced the outcomes of their work at a conference in Australia in 1998. The underlying principle of Google's PageRank algorithm is that is if a web page is important then it is pointed to by other important pages. This needs to be read carefully. It is not just the number of links but the links from important pages, and that means a great deal of analysis has to be performed on the results from the web crawls. This concept of reverse citation was not invented by Brin and Page but comes from the work of Eugene Garfield and his Science Citation Index which he developed in the late1950s. The mathematics of PageRank is very complex but the computational effort is perhaps greater and led Google to develop its BigTable. It was implemented in 2005 having taken seven man-years of research effort.

The combination of PageRank and BigTable is only part of the story. Google is constantly trying to improve search performance and has a team of over 10,000 staff in research and development, 40% of the total staff complement.

The end result is a very powerful web search capability but in using Google we sometimes forget just how much work we have to do to find the information we are looking for. Sometimes we strike lucky and the information is on the first page or two of results. On other occasions we may spend a considerable amount of time following false leads. It can be very instructive to start a stop-watch at the beginning of an important Google search to note just how long it took to reach a satisfactory conclusion.

For some years now Google has offered a search appliance for enterprise search. There is more about this appliance in Chapter 6, but for now the important take-away is that enterprise search is not about web pages, even in an intranet. Documents very rarely refer to earlier or related documents, and so the concept of PageLink does not work. Google do pack some innovative technology into the box but despite the label on the server casing it is not a packaged version of the web search technology. It may well be a good fit for an enterprise search application but has to be compared to other enterprise search products and not allowed to short-circuit the evaluation process just because it is sold by Google.

With Web Search You Have Options

Whenever you carry out a Google search there are always other options available, and you usually have a Plan B if you cannot find what you are looking for. Even if you find information on Google you will probably do a quick evaluation to see if you trust it, taking into account the web site, the age of the document, the formatting (a pdf always looks more impressive than a Word document) and perhaps the organization publishing the information.

In the case of enterprise search you have nowhere else to search. If you can't find a document you do not know if it is because it does not exist or because for some technical reason the search application cannot find it. In addition security management to ensure that users only gain access to documents that they have permission to see is of major importance.

Information Quality

Even Google cannot ensure that you are only presented with high quality information. Just because there are a lot of links to a page from an important site does not mean that the information is of high quality. Quality, like relevance, is relative and personal. If you have a poor quality document and cannot find anything better then miraculously the quality of the document you have in your hand improves considerably.

For the purposes of search it is not about the quality and accuracy of the document but also about the format of the document. Text information is often referred to as 'unstructured' information, but that is in comparison to the highly structured state of a relational database. Text has a structure that enables us to understand the meaning of sentences, but the structure of the document itself is of great importance in helping the search application to deliver relevant results.

Typical problems include the following:

Poor Titles

PowerPoint files are frequent culprits, with titles such as 'Project Prospero – update' with no indication of what the scope is of Project Prospero and the date of the presentation.

No Author Information

Many enterprise searches are about people. Now that you know Simon has been involved in Corporate Social Responsibility work you may want to find other documents that Simon has prepared. Simon is a member of the Governance Group but all the presentations are unnamed as the Governance Group knows exactly who prepared and gave the presentation, so why add a name?

Metadata

Good quality and consistent metadata is essential in achieving good quality search. In general searching a document management application is a delight because documents are set within folders and so acquire the basic folder metadata (e.g. FY2012/13) automatically. A document management system will often refuse to let a user file a document without adding certain metadata, such as their name, department, job title, and some subject terms. Web content added through a web content management system or documents added through SharePoint are a different matter. Metadata is explored in more detail in Chapter 7.

Ambiguous Date Formats

One of the most challenging metadata problems in enterprise search is the requirement to carry out date and date-range specific searches. The PowerPoint file on Project Prospero was finalized in June 2011 but one of the search results listed a 2012 version. This is because Simon wanted to change a couple of words in the presentation and then filed it away. This adds a 2012 date to the file metadata but for all practical purposes the document is identical to the 2011 version. The management of dates is something that is far more important in enterprise search than in web search.

Another challenge is that the date format for North America is month/day/year and for most of the rest of the world is day/month/year. Most search engines normalise the date to a common format so that it is possible to search for all documents published (or updated!) in March 2012. The complication arises when the results set out the date in the original date format.

Document Structure

It can also be helpful to ensure that documents have informative chapter headings and informative sub-headings. Even if the search application is not giving these weight as metadata remember that someone finding the document may want to scan through it at speed to find a particular piece of information.

Language

In the world of search text is not about the meaning of words but the meaning of sentences and the meaning of sections of documents.

Even within English the same word can have very different meanings. In the USA if you are asked to slate a meeting you know that you will need to set a date and perhaps the attendees and agenda. In the UK if you asked me to slate a meeting I'd ask you which meeting you wanted me to criticize. How can the same word have totally different meanings? The US usage is derived from a French word meaning 'to splinter', which is what slate does when it is mined. The UK social usage is derived from an Old Norse word 'sletta' meaning 'to slap'.

Understanding the meaning of social language is going to be increasingly important in the future as social media applications become widely adopted. The search application will need to be alert to acronyms, slang, and the use of shortened forms of names.

Searching for information in multiple languages is also going to be increasingly important, not only because of social media in a local language but because companies are beginning to appreciate that the concept of English as a corporate language is not consistent with an ethical approach to employees and their cultural values. An even bigger challenge is searching for information in documents that have been written in the author's second or even third language. When speaking in a second or a third language there is an opportunity for the speakers to check that they have correctly understood each other. That will not be the case for a written document.

Summary

The speed and performance of web search with Google and Bing set levels of expectation for enterprise search that cannot be met. It is not just about the technology but about the categories of content that are published on the web and that even something only marginally close to what we were looking for may be adequate. Enterprise search is also about searching for information in many different applications, not just in different servers, and that adds significantly to the scale of the problem. Nevertheless there are solutions available but the resources and skills of the search support team are perhaps even more important as a success factor than the technology. If we expect enterprise search applications to understand the way we use language to communicate and then to create a search query then we need to start talking the language of search.

Further Reading

You'll find some more information regarding the subject matter of this chapter in the "Further Reading" (page 156) section in Appendix A.

CHAPTER 3

Defining User Requirements

All effective systems are based on a good understanding of user requirements. "We want it to work like Google" is an aspiration and not a user requirement. In this chapter a range of approaches are suggested to help define user requirements. There is no single approach that is better than the others and usually a blend of several is required. However a balance needs to be kept. At one end of the spectrum is the Google approach, in which innovations are tested out on customers and if there is a positive reaction then the innovation becomes a Google product. Apple is at the other end of the spectrum. The late Steve Jobs commented that Apple needed to provide customers with what they wanted even though they don't know what this was.

One of the challenges of enterprise search is that almost everyone uses Google's public web search as the definition of best practice. In Chapter 2 I pointed out that this is not a useful approach to defining the requirements for enterprise search but any discussion about user requirements will almost inevitably migrate towards a discussion about Google.

The general lack of support for search invariably means that little attention is paid to defining user requirements, and all too often changes to either a user interface or the implementation of a new search application are largely based on anecdote and hearsay.

The value of user research is not just in defining the requirements for technology but also in setting a benchmark that can then be used in the future to prioritise search enhancement activities.

In this chapter some of the techniques that can be used to define user requirements are presented. These may help define perhaps 80% of what is required. The remaining 20% will only be discovered over time and some proportion of the 80% will be found not to be of value. This is because:

- The organization itself will change over time, giving rise to new requirements and making others less important.
- As users become competent in using the search application they will start to push the boundaries of what is on offer.
- Software upgrades will offer new search functionality.
- As new content sources are indexed additional functionality may be required to optimize search performance.

Fortunately search applications are well suited to being modified and enhanced to meet emerging requirements, unlike many other enterprise applications where a change in business practice may require substantial and costly changes to be made.

Information Seeking Models

For well over thirty years there has been a great deal of research into trying to understand how users go about seeking information. It is beyond the scope of this book to try and summarize all these models. Some of them have intriguing titles such as berry-picking, information foraging, information scent and orienteering. There is a good summary of these by Marti Hearst in her book Search User Interfaces, and Peter Morville takes a fresh and pragmatic view of information seeking in his book Search Patterns. Both books are in the Essential Search Library at the end of this book. What you will gain from reading about these information seeking models is that what is being attemped is the reduction of complex cognitive processes to a single process that can be evaluated in practice.

My contribution to the discussion about information seeking is rather simplistic. I refer to it as the Eureka! Triangle (see Figure 3-1).

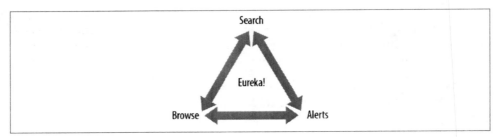

Figure 3-1. The Eureka! Triangle

When looking for information we will use the processes of browsing through the navigation of an intranet or folder structure of a document management system, of searching, and of being able to set up alerts either from RSS feeds or search profiles running in the background. These need to be kept in balance. In the case of intranets there can be such a focus on information architecture that when in usability tests someone uses search as an option the intranet team feel they have failed. The same applies to document management systems. Step outside to the web world, and organizations invest substantial amounts of money in designing home pages only to find that a significant number of site visitors arrive via Google and Bing and start deep inside the web site and possibly never see the wonderful carousel on the home page.

Another Search Engine! Why?

It is not unusual for an organization to have more than one search engine. The organization may have grown by acquisition, a major project justified having its own search engine and many enterprise applications will have embedded search functionality. There could also be clear business cases for eCommerce search on a web site and eDiscovery search for legal and compliance purposes. If there are existing search applications then the good news is that there will hopefully be some useful search logs and user experience. The bad news is that users will have found ways to get the best of the current search applications, and if search really is important to the organization there will be some reluctance to face the prospect of learning a new application.

Before any user requirement work is undertaken it is essential to have a good communications strategy that keeps everyone informed about the progress of the project. It could be that after a lot of user research the outcome is that there is no clear business case for an investment in a new search engine. As well as managing the expectations of all the stakeholders a news item on the intranet should make a point of inviting employees new to the organization to come forward and talk to the project team. The reasons are twofold. The induction period is always stressful and it is likely that newcomers have stress tested the current applications. The second reason is that they may have experience with other search engines and come with a different set of expectations about a good search experience.

User Requirements and User Satisfaction

The work carried out on defining user requirements is also of significant value in assessing search performance. From the outset the choice of a user research approach and the way that it is carried out should also take into account the potential use of the approach in search evaluation. If a survey of requirements is going to be conducted then the questions should be chosen so that at least some of them provide benchmarks for performance assessment in due course

Climate Surveys

Many organizations carry out what are often referred to as 'climate surveys' to assess the attitudes of staff towards culture, management approach and operational issues. These surveys are usually carried out annually and should include a question about whether employees feel that they can find the information they need to make decisions or carry out tasks. This is one good example of a metric that can be used to assess the post-implementation success of the search engine. If the current level of satisfaction is 60% there is certainly going to be room for improvement.

Diaries

Asking people to maintain a diary of their search experiences can provide valuable information, but the design of the diary sheet needs to be developed with care, and with some pilot trials. Expecting people to complete a diary on a daily basis for a period of time is not realistic. This is at best a dip-stick test to see if there are any outlier search requirements which have not been identified using other techniques.

The information that could be collected in diary entry would include:

- The reason for the search ("Needed to find the latest version of the security policy")
- The query used ("Security policy")
- How many results were returned?
- Were you successful in finding the information, and how long did it take you?
- If you were unsuccessful what did you do next?

The best way to get useful outcomes is to agree with volunteers perhaps just two days in a specific week they are going to use the diary, perhaps a day when they are planning an internal presentation or preparing a project report. A quick telephone call during the course of the day to be supportive will be welcomed by the volunteers as will a public acknowledgement of the role that they have played. These volunteers in particular would be a good set of participants in later proof of concept or implementation tests.

Focus Groups

It can be very tempting to run focus groups. The logic is that getting together a group of people who make extensive use of search would be a good way to start to develop a set of requirements. However it is highly likely that these people would be able to use almost any search engine and get the best out of it. Providing a good solution to people who find the current search application untrustworthy or difficult to use is just as important but it can be very difficult to find potential participants.

There is usually pressure from senior managers to set up some focus groups. These rarely have the desired effect as the participants may be unwilling to highlight problems that they find in obtaining and using information lest the other participants mark them down as incompetent. Running a focus group also requires two people, one to facilitate and one to record the comments, so some of the potential gains in interviewer time are already at risk. Then there is the challenge of making sure that all the participants turn up, so that the group is representative of a group of employees. Having someone miss the meeting and then insist on having an individual interview again wastes time and delays the conclusion of the project.

It is probably better to use focus groups later in the requirements-gathering process to validate some initial outcomes than to use them as an initial source of requirements.

The team at New Idea Engineering use 'Development Dollars" to prioritize requirements. They give the group $100 and ask them to buy the requirements that they need. They soon get the idea that budgets are limited and quickly allocate the $100 across perhaps just three or four requirements. The process itself can reveal a lot about the priorities of each of the members of the group that have not come out in the discussion phase of the group interview.

Help Desk Calls

A review of help desk calls is a very important part of the user requirements gathering, even if there has not been a specific search help desk in the past. The help desk tickets may reveal many points of failure, even if rarely points of success. It is also important to bear in mind that reducing calls to help desks is important in terms of employee satisfaction and help desk productivity.

Microsoft Product Description Cards

In 2002 Microsoft user experience researchers Joey Benedek and Trish Miner developed a set of 118 adjectives that could be used to define usability in test situations. These adjectives are often used in the initial stages of an intranet or web site implementation but are just as relevant in the early stages of defining search requirements.

Some of the adjectives in the list are directly relevant to search, including:

- Comprehensive
- Convenient
- Customisable
- Easy to use
- Fast

- Secure

The approach is especially useful when trying to understand the good and bad points about a current search implementation. There are various ways of using these terms in the process of starting to define user requirements. Ideally each word should be written on a card, and a set of cards given to small groups of users. The number in each group should be no more than five, because the objective is to get a discussion going about the terms that best describe the current search application, and the terms that should define the re-launched search. Initially each group should be asked to select eight cards for the current search application, and then in a second run for the new application. Once eight have been selected then the groups might be asked to bring the total down to five.

This approach is highly qualitative and its value is more in starting to gain the involvement of users than in developing a checklist of requirements based on the final outcomes of the card sorting tests.

It is possible to carry out this process remotely, just asking people to highlight the descriptions they have selected, but the best results are gained from a number of groups working together, presenting their results and then having a short discussion about the similarities and differences between the group results.

It is important to position this process as a 'fun' process which is just one input into defining the overall user requirements.

Personas

A widely-used technique in the design and development of web sites and intranets is the use of personas. A persona is a fictional person who represents characteristics of a group of people with similar requirements for information to undertake tasks.

Personas bring many overall user-focus benefits, including:

- Users' goals and needs become a common point of focus for the team.
- The team can concentrate on designing for a manageable set of personas knowing that they represent the needs of many users.
- By always asking, "Would Anne use this?" the team can avoid the trap of building what users ask for rather than what they will actually use.
- Design efforts can be prioritized based on the personas and so design and project creep can be managed
- Disagreements over implementation decisions can be sorted out by referring back to the personas.

- Implementations can be constantly evaluated against the personas, where appropriate using business end-users who were involved in the development of each of the personas.

The usability consultant Donald Norman sums it up well:

> Do Personas have to be accurate? Do they require a large body of research? Not always, I conclude. The Personas must indeed reflect the target group for the design team, but for some purposes, that is sufficient. A Persona allows designers to bring their own life-long experience to bear on the problem, and because each Persona is a realistic individual person, the designers can focus upon features, behaviors, and expectations appropriate for this individual, allowing the designer to screen off from consideration all those other wonderful ideas they may have. If the other ideas are as useful and valuable as they might seem, the designer's challenge is to either create a scenario for the existing Persona where they makes sense, or to invent a new Persona where it is appropriate and then to justify inclusion of this new Persona by making the business case argument that the new Persona does indeed represent an important target population for the product.

However be aware that intranet personas may not be appropriate to the requirements of enterprise search and it is advisable to develop a set of search personas which drill down into search requirements in more detail. Figure 3-2 shows one approach to segmenting user requirements into four broad categories, each of which could be represented by one or two personas.

The term 'current domain' is used both in an organizational sense (my current business unit) and in an expertise sense (I am a chemist). A novel domain could be someone moving to a new business unit, or taking on different responsibilities, such as a research chemist taking on a business planning role. Precision and recall should not be taken as absolutes but as indicating either a requirement for a few specific documents or for a much larger group of relevant documents.

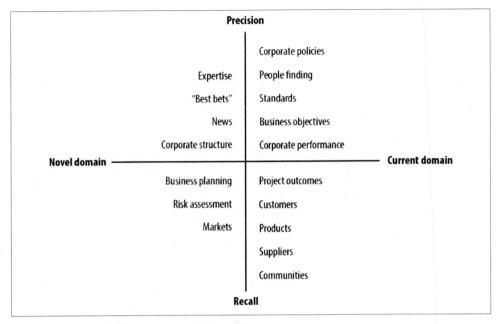

Figure 3-2. Four categories of user requirements

Team Meetings

One of the critical success factors in search is gaining an understanding the user context. Search logs may disclose what search terms have been used, but not why they were used.

Every organization has team meetings, though increasingly these are virtual team meetings, which require substantially more planning. Teams tend to have regular tasks, such as providing monthly status reports on new projects, revising corporate policies and tracking the activities of competitors. Sitting in on these meetings can help identify the types of searches that are carried out and what would be the desirable outcomes of the search process. The benefit of teams over focus groups is that team members will feel comfortable with each other and have a collective focus on certain corporate objectives which may well determine career development opportunities or compensation awards.

However there is no point just turning up at the meeting and asking for input on search requirements in the Any Other Business section of the meeting. The programme of attendances at the team meetings needs to be highlighted on the intranet. It is also important to have the discussion about search fairly high up on the agenda, so that it is positioned as an important topic. Having the discussion on the agenda also (hopefully!) ensures that attendees come prepared.

Of course, teams increasingly work and meet on a virtual basis, and this requires more preparation as the attention span of participants may well be lower when taking part in a meeting which may have been scheduled at a time that is not totally convenient for them. On the positive side as the attendees will be participating through a networked computer it may be possible for them to demonstrate some of the aspects of the current search application which they would like to see enhanced.

Always offer members of the team the option to talk individually about their search experience and requirements. They may not wish to disclose to their colleagues that they are having difficulty with the search applications

Usability Tests

Sadly in many organizations the resources to carry out usability studies are very limited, and often there are no corporate usability specialists. Work on the usability of the corporate web site may well have been outsourced. Using external expertise is not ideal for internal applications because a good understanding of the business is needed in both agreeing the tasks and interpreting the results.

There is a lot of debate about how many participants should be used for each test. Jakob Nielsen suggests that five participants will highlight most of the main issues with the search application, and for the purposes of gaining an indication of user requirements for the specification of a new search application that is probably a good number to aim for.

Use Cases

A use case is defined as a list of steps defining interactions between a user (sometimes referred to as the 'actor') and a system to achieve an objective. There is no 'correct' way to present a use case, and the use cases set out below are very informal ones. However they can be useful in starting to translate user requirements into a specification, something that is more difficult to do with personas. Any given employee may display many use cases.

The ten use cases set out below are very pragmatic, based on my observations of people at work in organizations. They are deliberately set out in alphabetical order as there is no single or set of use cases that are more common or more important than any of the others. The use cases have titles which should be recognizable in organizations.

Analysis

It is quite common in organizations to look for trends in performance, which could be financial, or measured in more complex Key Performance Indicators (KPIs). To undertake this analysis a user may want to find a defined set of reports, and some or all of these may contain a substantial element of numeric data. This is the area of content analytics and data/text mining, and on the edges of business intelligence.

Compliance

In this use case there is a requirement for high recall to verify that all the critical information has been identified. Although this is typical in a compliance situation it can also occur when there is a need to locate all the project reports on a defined project, or all the products that use a specific chemical over which there is a concern about poor quality standards

Expertise

The need to locate people, and in particular people with expertise, is often overlooked in designing search. All too often there are two search boxes, one for [search] and one for [people] which is unhelpful when the user is trying to find out about who knows someone, or even who knows which are the relevant documents. Many searches are carried out in an effort to find people with relevant expertise, and not just for the document itself.

Induction

In many organizations it is not unusual to have a staff turnover of more than 10% per annum, and there is sometimes a specific area of an intranet that supports early-stage induction into the organization. In addition there are many employees who will take on new roles and responsibilities during the year, perhaps in a different office or even in a different country. An important issue here is whether the search application will be able to provide some form of either a best bet so that the results of a search can be placed in context, and/or some tagging from other users which rates a document of being of particular value.

Item

The user's search will only be satisfied by finding a specific document, perhaps a presentation to a team or a project wrap-up document.

Learning

A feature of the learning persona is that the user is not at all sure about the best way to frame a search query. They may be seeking information on the work that the organization has undertaken to reduce its carbon footprint, and this could be covered by a very wide range of terms from corporate social responsibility to green engineering.

Mobile

The easy element of the Mobile persona is that the user will be using a screen format which is smaller than the average desktop. The more difficult elements are the authentication that may be required, the inability to print out the results of a search, single tasking resulting in the need to open a different application to read the item listed in the search results, and the way in which the query is formulated. This formulation could be heavily dependent on location if GPS is used as a background search criterion, something that may not be apparent to the user, or even useful if the implicit criteria is not relevant to the search.

Monitor

The main characteristic of this persona is that the search requirements are fairly consistent over a period of time, and the ability to be alerted to new information as soon as it has been indexed is usually very valuable.

Product

When a user is searching for information on a particular product or service, either as a basis for internal review or to meet the requirements of a supplier or customer, then a near miss is not good enough. If product code AC34-345-12 does not appear on the first page of search results then the user has a problem on their hands.

Task

Supporting standard tasks should be an important role for a search application, but few companies have any firm idea of what a task involves if it is not embodied in a workflow process. Understanding the information content of a task is going to be increasingly important in speeding the decision-making process and many organizations and search vendors are looking with considerable interest at search-based applications.

One-on-one interviews with employees can often uncover surprisingly complex tasks that depend on accessing multiple information sources. An example might be to set up a project team. This may require finding information on:

- The procedures for setting up a project

- Finding out if a project of this type, or for this client, has been carried out previously
- What forms need to be completed and forwarded to other departments
- Who the members of the project team should be
- The current availability of the prospective team members
- Internal guidelines on this particular type of project
- The project progress reporting procedures

User Interviews

It is very easy to spend time interviewing users and end up with little relevant information. This is because it can so easy to move away from the core subject of the interviews and get into specifics of design and content that are then difficult to scale up to a set of user requirements.

In setting up user interviews it is easy to think in terms of departments or roles, but in specifying search requirements some lateral thinking is called for.

Some important categories of users that are often overlooked in the interview programme include:

- Personal assistants to directors and senior managers
- Employees who have recently joined the organization, not just because they will be coping with the usual induction issues but also because they may have experience of how search is delivered in their previous organization
- Employees with a background in the sciences, law and medicine who will be familiar with large-scale information systems from their time at college, and during the course of their careers.
- Excellent advice can be found in Steve Portigal's book The Art and Craft of User Research Interviewing.

In conducting interviews I have found this diagram to be of value in getting the discussion going (see Figure 3-3).

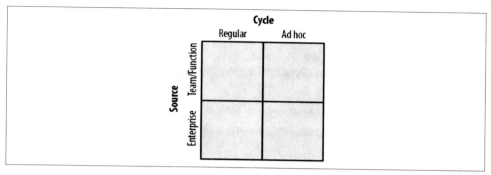

Figure 3-3. Cycle and source diagram

The objective is to gain an understanding of information gathering that is carried out on a regular basis (and could be supported by search alerts) and ad hoc requirements which are almost always carried out under time pressures. This diagram also distinguishes information which has been collected and is under the management of a team or department and the need to discover information that may be anywhere in the enterprise.

I encourage interviewees to write on the diagram and collect these together as I go along. In many cases the interviews have to be carried out by telephone and sending this diagram in advance with a brief description of its purpose enables me to get quickly into the interview without wasting time. It is possible to let a face-to-face interview extend to 50 minutes but a telephone conversation needs to be limited to 30 minutes.

User Surveys

Conducting user surveys with web-based survey tools has transformed the effort required to carry out large scale surveys and have the results available in a short period of time. There are some important guidelines that should be taken into account in designed the search survey:

- Start out with no more than ten questions, which will probably take a user around 10 minutes (or a cup of coffee) to complete. Anything longer will need very careful design.

- The questions should be intuitive, so that respondents gain an immediate understanding of why the question is being asked.

- Ideally provide an indication of how far through the survey a respondent has reached.

- Don't ask questions that rely on feats of memory about what the respondent did over a past period of time. 'Do you use search now more than you did a year ago?' has no value at all.

- Don't expect respondents to write essays in a text box. Invite respondents to contact you if they would like to talk through issues in more detail.
- Recognise that it may be better to send out different surveys to specific user groups than try to accommodate the views of the entire workforce with a single set of questions
- If using Likert or Likert-like surveys do not average out the scores. Use the median.
- Commit to summarizing the outcomes by a given date, and invite respondents to comment on the results.
- Test the survey, and then test it again.

For more guidance turn to Surveys That Work by Caroline Jarrett. As with user interviews there is a substantial body of good practice about the conduct of surveys. You are only going to do it once so it is advisable to do it properly. The future of the organization could depend on the outcomes.

Search Benchmarking

If the aim of an enterprise search project is to improve search performance it is important to benchmark the current application. Great care is required to ensure that the test searches that are carried out are directly comparable with those undertaken initially in the Proof of Concept tests (Chapter 9) and then after the implementation (Chapter 10). The search queries need to be 'real' queries, not just queries dreamt up over a cup of coffee by the project team. The content scope should also be defined; perhaps all documents associated with a particular project or product launch. This collection is sometimes referred to as the Gold Collection or Golden Collection as it will be used on a regular basis. Not only is this collection of value in benchmarking the current application against the new application but also to assess the impact of changes that are made to the ranking parameters.

Search benchmarking is especially important in the case of web site search, as here the competition is certainly going to be Google. Trying to implement a search application that is 'better' than Google is a waste of time unless you are prepared to invest the $10 billion that Google currently spends annually on research and development. In many organizations, such as universities, the web site is a core information resource but the queries that might be posted from academic and research staff are likely to be very different to those from prospective students.

Search Logs

Search logs are an invaluable source of user requirements, but they are covered in more detail in Chapter 10.

Stories

Stories about search successes and failures can be very powerful in supporting a business case but not in defining the functionality of the search application. Extrapolating from even a number of stories some specific features that are required is not sensible.

User Feedback

All search applications should encourage users to provide feedback on their search experience, be it good or bad. A simple form on the search home page that gives users an opportunity to write a brief comment is all that is needed. The form should automatically capture the query terms. Asking users to fill in a detailed questionnaire never works. Calling them personally to discuss the search outcomes always pays dividends.

Writing the User Requirements Report

Almost certainly what will emerge from this work is a classic 80/20 set of requirements; good agreement on the core requirements and quite a number of outliers. It is important to make sure that the reasons for these outlier requirements are fully understood. It is essential that the draft user requirements report is circulated widely, and certainly to anyone who was involved in any way with the user research. It may not be until these employees read the report that it becomes evident that one particular group feels they did not present their case clearly enough. Other readers, seeing the results, may be able to contribute additional insights, and perhaps a story that can be used for emphasis.

All this takes time. The overall schedule might go as follows:

Month 1:

Plan out the user research project and brief all those who will be involved about the objectives and scope of the research

Month 2 and Month 3:

Allow two months as a minimum for the user research. Setting up meetings with individual teams can often be a critical step in the timing as these may only happen on a monthly basis

Month 4:

Summarise the outcomes and check any anomalies before preparing the draft requirements report

Month 5:

Allow several weeks for a review by participants before concluding the user requirements work and writing the final report.

This suggests that work on the user requirements research probably needs to start six months before the process of writing the requirements for a new search application or for an enhancement to the current search application. This may seem quite an extended period of time but this is an application which could make a significant difference to the performance of everyone in the organization and the performance of the organization itself.

Summary

Your employees will search in many different ways. There could be one small user group to whom a search engine with a particular feature could have a significant impact on operational performance. The user experience with a search engine starts at the point that the user realizes that they need to find a piece of information and ends with the successful use of that piece of information to make a good decision. The range of use cases will mean that a range of different techniques are going to have to be employed, with consequences for the research schedule and for the resources needed. As far as possible use techniques that can be used to measure the success of the implementation. Above all remember the adage that if it can't be measured then it can't be managed.

Further Reading

You'll find some additional information regarding the subject matter of this chapter in the "Further Reading" (page 156) section in Appendix A.

CHAPTER 4

Planning for Search

Given the potential benefits and challenges of enterprise search it is surprising that the 2012 Findwise Enterprise Search and Findability survey indicated that only 14% of respondents had a search strategy, though 30% were planning to develop a strategy in 2012/2013. This result is consistent with the Digital Workplace Trends report from Net-StrategyJMC and tends to support the view that search is not seen as a business-critical element.

Search does need to be planned. It is technically challenging, users have both high expectations and a high dependency on the success of search and there is going to need to be a substantial investment in personnel for the search support team. As you read through this book you will find there is just one single theme. I call it White's Rule of Search Investment:

> The impact of search on business performance depends more on the level of investment in a skilled team of people to support search than it does on the level of investment in search technology.

There is a corollary:

> Without an investment in a skilled team of people to support search no matter how great the investment is in search technology there will be no impact on business performance.

Enterprise search also bumps into many business operations. The search engine will need to interface with other applications and there are some legal and compliance issues. In the future the boundaries between search, business intelligence and content analytics are going to become increasing blurred and delivering access to enterprise search through mobile devices is going to be essential within a year or so.

In this chapter some of the business and technology issues that need to be addressed in a business plan and search strategy document are set out.

Making a Business Case

If you are asked to make a business case for enterprise search based on a financial Return-On-Investment model of just the costs associated with the software take heed of two important pieces of advice. The first is that it shouldn't be done and the second is that it can't be done.

When I am initially asked to help an organization make an ROI case for investing in enterprise search my initial request is to see business cases for other enterprise applications where the investment has been justified using an ROI calculation. Usually no such business case exists, or where it does the calculation is based on vague assumptions and yet approval is given for the investment. The justification is usually based on the proposition that without the investment the organization will not be able to function, supported by the signature of someone on the Board of the organization. Sadly at present no one on the Board wishes to be the sponsor for enterprise search and knows little about the technology itself or the value of the technology to the organization. The request for an ROI is purely a defensive measure in case things go wrong down the line.

Search is a high-touch application. It will be used personally by a substantial proportion of all employees in a service business and even in a manufacturing business enterprise search will support decisions being made which affect even staff on a production line. This cannot be said for a finance system, a customer relationship management system or a treasury management system, as just three examples.

The main reason why an ROI cannot be calculated is that there are no standard processes involved such as entering an invoice or updating an HR system. These processes can (at least in theory) be timed and costed based on the salary and overheads of an employee, but that is not the case with search. There is some published research from International Data Corporation which suggests employees spend perhaps eight hours a week looking for information. Making assumptions about the time that could be saved by investing in a good search application will not be founded on any sort of reality.

The reality is that if an organization needs a financial ROI to make an investment in search then it fails to appreciate the value of information as an asset, and in addition thinks that there is just a single metric on which to judge the business case for search. In fact there are multiple business cases, probably the same as the number of use cases set out in Chapter 3. Search has to be seen within the overall context of the business and its objectives, and that is why a full business plan is needed for search.

Invest in Skills Before Software

Over the last couple of years much of the investment in collaboration applications has been justified on the basis that the organization is not working together as effectively as it should, and implementing a collaboration application will transform the situation.

There is usually only anecdotal evidence about poor collaboration and in due course only anecdotal evidence about improvement. When it comes to search the situation is the same. Someone (usually senior) has complained that they cannot find anything with the current search application and the organization needs to get something better.

Almost without exception if the organization is using a search application that has been implemented in the last five years, all the upgrades installed, and all the bugs fixed then significant benefits will arise from increasing the size and skill base of the search support team. During the course of writing this book I was involved in helping a major UK university achieve a higher level of satisfaction with their web site search application. There was virtually no internal support. One developer occasionally took time out to have a look at the search logs, but did not have the time to do anything more. I discovered that another UK university was using the same search application and were very pleased with the performance. The difference? Two members of the web team were allocated full-time to web site search.

Search Support Team

Technology can be bought but a search support team needs to the sort of people who are in very short supply inside most companies. Most of Chapter 10 is about the skills needed in a search team. It would not be too much of an overstatement to say that if you cannot find the people who will form the search support team there is really no point in making any investment in an enterprise search application.

To summarize Chapter 10 there are five search team roles:

- Search Manager taking management responsibility for search delivery
- Search Technology Manager, looking after the IT elements
- Search Analytics Manager, running and analyzing search logs
- Search Information Specialist, with responsibility for search quality
- Search Support Manager, providing training and user support

In the initial stages of an enterprise search project these roles could be undertaken alongside other work but once the implementation begins these roles need to be filled on a full time basis. There simply is no option. If senior managers say that this is a ridiculous number of people to be supporting a single application ask how many staff support the ERP, business intelligence and document management applications. None of these are used by almost every member of staff every day.

Stakeholder Analysis

The term 'stakeholder' is common parlance in organizations but usually little is done to analyze them in any formal sense. The matrix (see Figure 4-1) below can be useful in this respect.

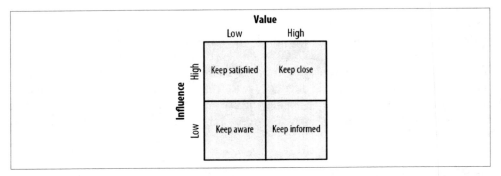

Figure 4-1. The value and influence matrix

The first step in creating this matrix is to brainstorm a list of potential stakeholders and for each group, or individual, define the following elements:

- Name and position
- Potential positive and negative impacts on the project (Influence)
- What would the project expect the stakeholder to contribute (Influence)
- What is the stakeholder's expectation of the outcome of the project (Value)

Once the stakeholders have been plotted onto the matrix the stakeholder strategy starts to take shape. For the High Influence/High Value quadrant (General Manager?) a member of the project team should build and maintain a one-to-one relationship. The High Value/Low Influence quadrant would have intranet management, document management and records management teams. These teams need to be kept informed and their views brought into the discussions of the project team. The classic example in the High Influence/Low Value quadrant would be the entire IT department and these need to be reassured that it is in their interests to be supportive. Finally in the Low Influence/Low Value quadrant would come the managers of most corporate departments who already have a lead application (finance, marketing etc). The 'keep aware' strategy is a blend of keeping them informed on a regular basis and be aware if they start to have concerns about the direction of the search project.

As the project proceeds some of the stakeholders may need to be moved to a different quadrant, but the maximum effort needs to be expended on identifying the stakeholders in the high value quadrants and delivering on their expectations.

Business Impact

It is important to set out the objectives of the organization as these could have a major influence on the way that search develops. The acquisition strategy is especially important as this could require the search application to index substantial new repositories at short notice and also result in the negotiation of new license deals with a number of different vendors. There could be challenging divergences in metadata values and consistency.

One way of identifying ways in which the search application could support the business is to review the risks that are almost always published in the annual report, and work up a mitigating approach to each risk that involves the search application. In 2011 Hofmann La Roche, one of the world's leading pharmaceutical companies, identified five simple but challenging questions that employees were probably asking themselves and colleagues on a regular basis:

- Can I handle this?
- What is the implication?
- Can we find out sooner?
- Will it work?
- Have I chosen wisely?

If enterprise search can provide answers to those questions then the business case can be made on just a few pieces of paper.

As well as this top-down approach the techniques set out in the previous chapter will provide all the evidence that is needed as to how search can have an impact on business operations and the achievement of objectives.

Even though search is used very widely in the organization it is virtually impossible to make a convincing business case across all, or at least, most employees. It is advisable to build the overall business case for investment on a number of individual business cases that resonate with senior managers. These might include improving customer service, shortening the time to prepare business proposals, reducing the time to develop a new product or being more responsive to the actions of competitors. The metrics that will illustrate success will be different for each of these business cases but will be grounded in business processes.

Nothing carries more weight than a story from a respected manager about how they failed to find information that could have made a positive impact on the organization. It's a trick used by many management authors, who use call-out stories to make an impact in an otherwise mundane book on some aspect of business operations. Beginning the business case document with a really strong search success or search failure (or both!) is a guarantee that readers of the business plan will already be pre-disposed to agree to the investment.

The 2012 Findwise survey found that the top ten justifications for enterprise search implementation were the following, based on a summation of respondents ranking these reasons as 'imperative' or 'significant'. The list is in decreasing order of importance:

- Accelerate retrieval of information from known information sources
- Improving the re-use of information and knowledge
- Increasing the extent of collaboration through finding people with relevant expertise
- Eliminating information silos and the risk that important information was not being found and used
- Accelerating the speed of finding people both by name and expertise
- Raising the awareness of what was already known
- Eliminate duplication of work because relevant information could not be found
- Improving the consistency and quality of response to queries from customers and partners
- Creating a more personalized intranet solution
- Providing support for compliance management

Unfortunately none of those are easy to quantify.

Search Owner

If building a search team is difficult finding someone who will take business responsibility can be even harder. This is probably because there are no business and compliance-critical workflow processes that are supported by enterprise search. Look around at the main enterprise systems and they are owned by the manager responsible for the workflow; Sales Director, Operations Director, HR Director and so on. In around 70% of organizations (based on the Findwise survey) the decision on a search application and the management of the application are the responsibility of the IT department. In many organizations search is owned by Corporate Communications, almost certainly when the same search application is being used for the web site and for internal enterprise search.

Here are two questions for you. In your organization what percentage of the total amount of content being indexed is owned by either Corporate Communications or IT and what percentage of the total number of employees work in IT and Corporate Communications? The answers will be small numbers, almost certainly less than 10%. IT should be delivering support services and certainly have an important role in search sub-system performance management. When the day comes that IT people regularly attend meetings with business units with supplier and customer facing staff then IT can own search. But not until that day.

In an ideal world search should report to the senior manager whose performance bonus is based on meeting customer requirements, either through product development and delivery or service development and delivery. This could be a General Manager, or Director of Manufacturing. All that the search owner really needs to do is fight for a sensible capital and operating budget.

Content

A search engine needs to be instructed about the content that needs to be indexed. The place to start is a content audit based around the repositories of information that the organization holds. The content audit needs to cover the following elements for each repository and application.

Owner

The first, and often most difficult, step is to find out who owns the repository. It may have been set up some time ago and the initial owner might even have left the company. If there is a current owner the chances are that the original intention of the repository has long since been overridden. This is often the case with a departmental repository where the department has been merged or fragmented over time.

Scope

A brief description of the content should be prepared, along with a description of the user categories who contribute and use the information in the repository. The total file size and total number of documents are important to know when it comes to sizing the search application. For the same reason the rate of addition of documents by time will give an indication of how frequently the repository needs to be re-indexed, or whether the documents are such that they need to be indexed as soon as they are added to the repository.

Document Size and File Formats

All the file extensions should be identified and listed out and at a minimum the maximum file size of the collection should be ascertained.

Metadata Management

If the content has been contributed through a content management or document management application then there will probably be good metadata tagging. If it is just a shared file server then even basic folder metadata could be inconsistent.

Language

Making the assumption that all the content is in a single language and that the language is English is only a safe assumption in a very few countries of the world. It could be that the French version of a document has been stored alongside the English version in what otherwise looks like a totally English-language collection.

Security

Working out the security rights is essential, and like so many other elements in the audit list it may not be immediately obvious what these are, especially if they are at document level rather than server access level.

The work involved in undertaking this content audit should not be under-estimated. In the process of converting this list into an Excel database any cell that is not completed could mean that the content is not indexed, or not indexed properly, and so becomes invisible.

Technology

An important component of the technology section is to provide a list of current applications that already have search functionality, possibly as an embedded application. Examples might include document management and records management systems and enterprise resource planning systems. There are often more of these embedded search applications than most managers appreciate. These are often optimized for a specific application, and probably an enterprise application could not provide the same level of search performance and satisfaction. Having a list of these applications enables decisions to be made about whether there would be a benefit in providing a federated search environment.

There are a number of technologies that need to be surfaced in a search business plan, and these include:

- The use of open-source software
- Mobile access to enterprise information assets
- The adoption of cloud/software-as-a-service applications
- In-house versus external development and maintenance

In most organizations there will already be a number of search applications in use. It is easy to suggest that having just one powerful engine will solve all current search problems at a stroke. It could easily add to them. An important section of any business plan should set out how the process of migration from a number of different search applications to one single enterprise search application is going to be accomplished. This is not just a technology issue, but has to be approached both from an IT and a user perspective. Without doubt there will be some considerable change management, training and support issues that will have to be addressed and solutions put in place long before the technical migration occurs and for some time afterwards.

As with any software application a search vendor will release versions of the software to either address bugs or to provide additional functionality. This section of the business plan should set out the basis for considering whether to implement a new version of the software, bearing in mind that there could be risks with connectors to other applications.

Infrastructure

Enterprise search can have some challenging infrastructure requirements as far as storage in particular is concerned. The topology of a large-scale enterprise search application with good disaster recovery and the minimum latency on queries will need careful planning. The issues will not just be about the size of the index relative to the size of the repository but also the write speeds of the disk arrays. Many capacity planning specialists will be in novel territory when it comes to planning search capacity.

Almost certainly there will be a need for test, development and production servers. For large-scale enterprise search applications there will need to be multiple production servers with distributed indexes.

Network bandwidth to distant but still important offices can also present issues that need careful review. Substantial files could be downloaded very rapidly for perhaps 10-15 minutes as a user works their way through the top 50 results looking for a specific piece of information. This can be a particular issue with PowerPoint files, and a number of vendors offer a feature to render the document, or PowerPoint file, as a small HTML thumbnail image.

Disaster Recovery

It is tempting to put search down the bottom of the disaster recovery priority list but arguably it should be right at the top. It may enable the organization to keep going while other applications are brought back to life. After all the search index will contain a copy of most, if not all, of the information that the organization possesses, and if the application can provide users with an HTML thumbnail of a document that could be more than enough for business-as-usual to continue.

A disaster recovery plan usually sets outs a Recovery Time Objective (RTO) defining the maximum application downtime and a Recovery Point Objective (RPO) noting an acceptable restore point. For an enterprise search application these need to be considered from basics rather than the blind adoption of objectives from other enterprise applications. It is not just a case of getting the application back and running from a user perspective but understanding and accounting for content that may not have been completely crawled or an index that has not been correctly updated. The index itself may have been distributed around the world, and with disaster recovering will come the need to re-synchronize the indexing process.

Security

Organizations are rightly very concerned about the risks from employees finding information that they are not entitled to see. Even if there is a corporate security policy the questions that should be asked is whether it is granular enough and implemented rigorously enough to ensure that ACLs can be created and maintained. The potential impact on staff and the reputation of the organization from a failure of the security policy could be very dramatic.

This is especially the case if the document being created is being indexed as soon as it is saved to a repository. At that moment in time there is in effect a duplicate of the content accessible to anyone with the correct security permissions. The index will almost certainly be backed up on a second server for disaster recovery purposes. Removing the document from the repository will almost certainly not remove the content from the index. If the document was a list of senior executive salaries then a search for this information might well disclose the amounts even if the document has been deleted.

Performance

There are many ways of measuring search performance. User-centric measurements are set out in Chapter 10 but and certainly need to be summarized in the business plan. In addition there are also some system performance measures that need to be set out. These typically include:

- The optimum freshness for all categories of content
- Crawl times and crawl frequency
- The rate at which content is going to have to be ingested in order to achieve the desired freshness
- The latency between ingestion and the index being updated
- The amount of temporary disk space used in the process of creating and updating the index

- Total size of the index as a percentage of the total amount of content
- Elapsed indexing time for a new content set
- Indexing processor time, which excludes speed gains from parallel processing
- The expected number of queries-per-second
- Desired response times

In cases where the enterprise search application is also going to be used for site search on the corporate web sites the internal performance and external (public) performance metrics may be quite different.

When desired response times are being established a number of special cases need to be taken into consideration. Federated search will almost certainly be slower than searching on a single repository or application and the way in which security management has been implemented will also have an impact on search response times. The time taken to display a results set on the desktop is only a small element of the search process, and users will quickly become dissatisfied with any response time to open up a document in excess of perhaps 10 seconds. This latency time is not just absolute but relative. If one search provides a user with response times of only a few seconds and the next search takes perhaps 30 seconds to call up a document the user reaction will be one of considerable disappointment even if in absolute terms the search application is working to the maximum of its technical performance.

Metadata and Taxonomies

A few years ago at a search conference there was a presentation about a new search implementation. The search manager reported that one of the tests that had been run during the implementation was to find members of staff called Jane. To everyone's surprise most of the high relevance results were to male employees. It turned out that they had all written and submitted their cvs on a template owned by someone called Jane, and the search engine was placing more value on this metadata item than on the name field.

The problem with metadata is that the content contributor has to add it, and does so either with reluctance, or without due care or a combination of both conditions. This section of the search strategy needs to highlight the importance of metadata and how it will be generated, either automatically (e.g. the name of the content contributor from the system log-in information) or through manual addition. Entity extraction is a half-way house.

All the evidence points to the benefit of a taxonomy and metadata enhancing search performance, and especially in presenting highly-relevant information. However taxonomies are time-consuming to compile and to maintain. As with so many search-related issues a balance needs to be established between the value of the taxonomy and the benefit to users, taking into account that the users of the information may not be the people who have to add the taxonomy metadata in the course of saving the document.

Help Desk

A search application needs its own help desk, even if it is a virtual one, and there needs to be a Service Level Agreement both ways between the IT and Search Help Desks because it may take quite a bit of effort to work out what is causing the problem and what actions should be taken to remedy the problem.

Usability

Despite the high profile efforts of usability experts such as Jakob Nielsen few organizations seem to take usability seriously. Search usability testing is especially important because of the complexity of many search user interfaces with a profusion of filters, facets, annotations to results and perhaps even graphical representations of clusters of search results.

Training and Support

The view is sometimes taken that search should be so intuitive that there should be no need to providing training and support. This view is often based on the 'simplicity' of the Google search box, a view that ignores that books have been written on the very wide range of hacks that are available to users of Google search.

The same is true of an enterprise search application. Certainly there should be as few barriers as possible to carrying out a basic search, but in an enterprise context there are probably very few basic searches as finding most, and ideally all, of the relevant information is very important.

Risks

It is always advisable to have a risk management strategy for enterprise search, and this probably needs to cover off the following risks:

- Lack of resources in the search team leading to poor search performance
- Search manager leaves and there is no internal candidate
- Search vendor is acquired or goes out of business
- Search vendor unable to provide an adequate level of support
- No clear roadmap for development

- Changes in senior management at the vendor result in a repositioning of the search engine
- Inadequate security management leads to a breach of access permissions
- Key development skills in the open-source contractor are not available
- Disaster recovery procedures prove to be inadequate
- Enterprise networks are giving rise to significant performance problems
- Poor performance of connectors and APIs
- Best bets are no longer best bets

Web Site Search

An enterprise search strategy should also include a strategy for web site search. The major issue here will be whether using a search application optimised for internal information will be a good solution for external users of corporate web sites. There is no right answer. The requirements of both need to be defined and then the extent of the overlap and the implications of any compromises that might arise from using the same search application need to be considered.

Summary

Writing an enterprise search strategy or a business plan is not an exercise that can be completed in a few days sitting at a desk. Of the list of topics covered in this chapter the most time consuming will be the content audit. I find it difficult to understand why organizations do not document their search strategy, and then maintain it on at least an annual basis. As with any major IT project the more work undertaken in the planning stages the lower the risk and the greater the benefits post-implementation.

Further reading

You'll find some additional information regarding the subject matter of this chapter in the "Further Reading" (page 156) section in Appendix A.

CHAPTER 5

Search Technology Part 1

There are two fundamental components of any search application. An index of documents is created and then a search query is made which identifies which of those documents satisfies the enquiry. If only that was all there was to search process. The reality is that any search application consists of a set of modules, each of which carries out a specific task in the search process. Some of these modules may be bought in by the search vendor and others will be developed internally. The same is true of open-source software development.

Users should not have to know anything about search technology to be able to use it effectively but understanding the elements of search technology is important in the selection, testing and management of a search application. This is because one or more of these modules may be especially important in being able to meet a specific user requirement. It is very much a question of the whole only being as strong as the weakest link in the chain. If there are some limitations in the way that content is indexed then it does not matter how elegant the user interface looks information will be not able to be found that could be critical to the operations of the business.

To risk a generalization most other enterprise applications are built around a structured database with highly structured data collected through a well-established set of business processes. The data are collected using forms, data entry screens or from sensors of various types. It is usually relatively easy to track down where a problem has arisen. With search the issues are all about fuzziness and approximations, and tracking down why a particular document has not appeared high up on the list of relevant documents for a specific search can be very difficult to work out.

In this Chapter the building blocks of every search engine are described in sequence. In Chapter 6 some of the more complex functionalities are described and it is usually these functionalities which will be the basis for differentiating between potential vendors.

Content Gathering

A search application gathers in the information to be indexed in a number of ways. It can crawl through web pages and file servers, applications can be set up in a way that any new information is automatically sent to the search application for indexing, and RSS feeds can also indexed. Decisions have to be made about which servers are going to be indexed and at what frequency. In an ideal world it would be good to index information the moment that it is added to a server but this is not practical for two reasons. The first is that many applications auto-save as a document is being created and without careful management multiple versions of the same document may be indexed. The second is that crawling and indexing is bandwidth and processor intensive and both have cost implications.

All crawlers are not created equal. If information is missed or incorrectly passed back to the indexer no about of subsequent processing is going to find it. This is one of the major implementation issues, because the Proof of Concept make work well but as the scope of the collections to be indexed increases the chances of crawler failure increase substantially.

Another approach is to write a script for a server which identifies when a new document is added to the server (or an existing document is updated) and this is then pushed to the indexing engine of the search application for processing.

Once the search application has indexed a document and knows its location it will assume that the location does not change and that the document is always accessible. Locations do change and work then needs to be carried out to make sure that the new location is recorded in the search application. The document may not always be accessible as the server may have failed in some way or been taken down for service. This is when companies discover holes in disaster recovery plans, as it may not be obvious to a local IT manager that business-critical information is resident on a particular server.

A criterion for search performance is 'freshness', which is a measure of the time taken to update the index from the point at which the document was added to a repository. It is easy just to think that only news items needing to be added to the index as quickly as possible, but it could be just as important to add project reports so that the expertise gained is available with the minimum delay to an engineer who might be able to make use of information from that project to make a very competitive bid for a new customer.

Connectors

In enterprise installations the information to be indexed resides on a number of different application servers. For example the intranet may just be on a single web server but the people search application is on an Oracle HR application. To index the Oracle HR application may require the use of a connector. The best way to think of the role of a connector is to see it as a sophisticated travel plug. Instead of being able to use European power plugs in the USA the connector enables the content of the Oracle database to be read by the search application. Most search applications will come with a number of connectors integrated into the software but these will not cover every eventuality.

Connectors also tend to be version specific, so that a change in the version release of the Oracle HR application could require a new connector to be installed and tested. Connectors can be expensive to purchase and need constant attention to make sure that they are working correctly. They also connect applications developed by two different vendors and tracking down where the problems lie if the connector seems not to be working correctly can be a difficult discussion which has to be managed by getting the appropriate experts from both vendors around the same table. It can be very time-consuming.

Document Filters and Language Identification

Very rarely will the information be contained in plain text. Microsoft Office documents could be stored in many different versions of Office, and the Office suite also includes Excel spread-sheets, PowerPoint presentation files and perhaps Visio process diagrams. Then there are PDF files and Lotus Notes databases to be considered. Each document format has to be reduced to plain text, with any non-content control characters (such the code that produces justified text in Microsoft Office) being removed. 'Plain text' is actually a misnomer because although documents are often referred to as 'unstructured' information a document does contain a great deal of structure, such as a title, date, author, summary, contents page and index. A search engine will be able to place a different weight on words that appears in a title or executive summary to words appearing in the body of the document, so it is important to be able to retain core elements of the document structure.

Some document formats are more difficult to manage than others. An example would be a PDF version of an Excel spread-sheet where it is important to retain the row and column information, without which the document might just be converted into a set of cells without any context. Microsoft Visio and Microsoft Project files can also be a challenge. If it is important to be able to find people working on projects by indexing Microsoft Project files this requirement needs to be highlighted in the early stages of defining the scope of the search application.

Not all the content will be in English. Even in the UK it could also be in Welsh. The ways in which an search application will detect the language of the information are quite complex but at least the search application does have a significant amount of content to work with. The problem is much more challenging with queries. Is a query about 'sante' (the word for 'health in French) related to someone looking for articles in French on the subject of health or a mis-spelling of Santa, as in Sante Fe or event Santa Claus! Many international organisations have two different acronyms for their titles, notably the Organisation for Economic Co-operation and Development (OECD) which in French is l'Organisation de Coopération et de Développement Économiques (OCDE).

Parsing and Tokenising

This is the point in the process where the complexities of language have to be addressed by the search application. The text file output from document conversion now has to be converted into tokens by a process known as either parsing or tokenizing. In most cases each word is a token, but hypens, apostrophes and capital letters are just some of the problems an search application has to deal with. Is the name McDonald the same as MacDonald? From the point of view of the person concerned certainly not, but a user may only have heard the name mentioned in a conversation and might not know how the person's name is spelt. The search application should be able to offer the user the option of using either a specific spelling, reminding the user that there are two different spellings or allowing the user to query for M?cDonald in which ? is a so-called wild card that could be an 'a' or could be nothing at all. The parsing process has to be good enough to ensure that any valid query term can be matched to its position in the search application index.

The chances of doing this to perfection at the time the search application is installed are very low indeed, and this is just one of the reasons why there has to be a search support team looking through the search logs to identify where there seems to have been a mismatch between a query and the parsing process.

Other examples include:

- Hyphenated forms of words, for example to ensure that a search for oil-free compressors also finds documents where the word has been written as 'oilfree'
- Numbers, especially where they may refer to products
- Periods in abbreviations such as OCED and IMF
- Capitalized words, where apple and Apple have different meaning, though of course if 'apple' is the first word in a sentence then it will be Apple

The critical issue about tokenizing is that it has to match the query transformation. If 'I.B.M.' is converted into IBM but a query on I.B.M does not transform to IBM then no match will be made. One of the tasks at both implementation and later is to identify acronyms and other terms where the tokenizing rules and the query transformation rules may not meet in the middle.

Stop Words

In all languages there are many words that do not have any value as subject terms, such as 'the', 'of', 'for' and 'about' in English and these can be stripped out of the index though the saving in storage is not significant. Search application vendors either generate their own dictionaries of stop words or buy them in from a specialist supplier. Care needs to be taken that what seems to be a word of no value, such as 'next', is considered in the context of the business. In the UK there is a store group called Next which uses 'next' as its brand name. A stop list that removed this word would be a disaster for any company that did business with Next.

The classic example of need to be careful about a stop word list is the phrase from Shakespeare's play Hamlet "To be or not to be", which consists of words that would normally be defined as stop words.

In enterprise applications it is very easy to overlook the use of special characters, in particular punctuation which is used for product numbers or project codes. As with all aspects of search the way that the index is managed needs to match the way that the query is transformed or there will be no match.

Stemming and Lemmatization

These are two slightly different approaches to group together words that have a common stem. A user searching for 'ships' may also be interested in results on 'shipping' so the stemmer has to reduce both to 'ship' but also tag the occurrence in the index so that when the result is displayed the words are shown in their full form. The original work on stemming was carried out at the University of Cambridge in by Dr. Martin Porter in 1979. He developed an algorithm that enables a computer to undertake the stemming process through a set of rules. He later developed a specific version of this algorithm for English, known both as Snowball and Porter2.

This algorithm, with some small modifications, works well for all Romance languages, but other languages (such as Finnish or Arabic) pose additional problems. Good stemming is essential to reduce the frustration of the user when they are presented with results that seem to match the query term but have actually no relevance at all. The English language does not help in having so many synonyms which have very different meanings.

Porter's approach is based around a set of rules, and is sometimes described as affix-removal but there If is also a statistical approach that uses a very large corpus of text to derive a morphology for a language. The advantage of this approach is that it can be used for almost any language. However the challenges of stemming non-European languages are considerable.

Lemmatization refers to the use of a vocabulary and morphological analysis of words, to remove inflectional endings only giving the base or dictionary form of a word which is known as the lemma.

There is much discussion about which of the many approaches to stemming and lemmatization works best in providing good search effectiveness but without any definitive outcomes. When selecting a search engine there is no point in stipulating the stemming and lemmatization approaches that are required, but it is important to consider whether there are some common terms used in the organization which might give rise to frustration over seemingly relevant documents being presented which in fact are irrelevant. For example the use of 'gas' for 'petrol' in the USA makes life difficult for international oil companies who inevitably are also in the gas business.

It is also important to look ahead in the search implementation when the initial search implementation, which will almost certainly be on English language documents, is extended to other languages. Even if there is no immediate intention of searching for documents in Russian there should be a comfort factor in knowing that the search engine can process Russian language content and that at the Proof of Concept stage including Russian language content would be advisable.

Dates

Date management is important in enterprise search, especially in multi-national companies which have offices in both the North America and Europe. ISO Standard 8601 sets out the sequence as yyyy – mm – dd, and time as hh-mm-ss using the 24 hour clock. Many enterprise searches involve looking for the most recent document, or a document issued within a particular time period, or the first time a document was issued. The initial challenge is that many documents do not have fixed dates. A document can go through many versions, each of which has a different date and time, and the most recent may not be the latest released/approved version.

A very common problem is that normal practice in North America is to write the date in a mm-dd-yyyy or mm-dd-yy format, so that 5/3/12 is 3 May 2012. In the most of the rest of the world that date representation would be interpreted as 5th March 2012. Most search engines normalize dates to the ISO standard but the issue then is how the date is displayed in the search results. Ideally it should be as either dd-mmm or mmm-dd, both of which are unambiguous. This may seem a very small detail and not worth two paragraphs but it can cause very major problems in finding a specific document containing time-dependent information, such as month-end sales results.

Phrases

Many search queries are phrases. Corporate social responsibility was used as an example in Chapter 2 for this reason. Phrases are often tagged by the search application to identify if the words in a phrase are nouns, verbs, adjectives or other parts of speech. Vendors build up these databases from working with customers and by buying in phrase dictionaries. However this approach can also slow down the query process and there are a number of other approaches that can be used. As the index knows the proximity of every word in a document to every other word it can match the phrase just through a proximity analysis.

Phrases also bring us into the world of n-grams. Any sequence of two words is described as a bigram and three words as a trigram. N-grams are of fundamental importance in many aspects of the search process, especially in the management of search across multiple languages but a detailed description of their roles is outside the scope of this book.

Processing Pipeline

A number of search vendors refer to this collection of content processing steps as the content pipeline or the processing pipeline. The concept of a processing pipeline comes from software engineering where the output from one process becomes input of the succeeding process. The sales pitch tends to be around the speed and efficiency with which the content processing can be carried out because each step of the process has been optimized for the steps immediately before and after any given step.

In principle this is good news, especially for implementations where there is a significant number of new documents added each day. An example might be transcripts of call centre conversations. It does mean that upgrading or customizing one particular step may have some implications for other steps in the process.

Building and Managing the Index

Search applications use an inverted index to store all the tokens and other metadata generated by text processing. In principle an inverted index is the same as the index to a book, but instead of just giving a page number it is capable of not only telling the reader that the word 'intranet' is on page 23 but that it is the 3rd word on line 4. Similarly there could be an entry for 'strategy' on page 23 as the 4th word on line 4, so there would be a strong possibility that the page, if not the document, is about intranet strategy. If the entry for 'strategy' was on p22 as the 7th word on line 5 then that possibility could be smaller. This is a very simple example but it illustrates the point that search inverted indexes contain a significant amount of positional information.

There are two components of the index, a document-level index and a word-level index. The word-level index with its positional information is described in the previous paragraph. The document level index is a count of the number of occurrences of the term in the document.

Search applications have to cope with a significant amount of processing. There needs to be very fast random access to any point in the index, and indeed to multiple points at the same time. The index is also a very dynamic database. The number of changes to the HR database even in a very large company will be a very small percentage of the total number of records held in the database. Adding new employees usually means that they are replacing employees who have left the company, though even in tough economic conditions there will also be some new employees. Overall the rate of growth of the database will be fairly small.

That will not be the case with a search index. Each day each employee might spend an hour a day creating content that will need to be indexed, and that excludes emails. All that information has to be processed and indexed on a timely basis. Performance management for a search application is very important indeed, and each vendor will have their own approaches to the ordering of the index, and the way in which new (or changed) information is incorporated into the index. Users are very intolerant of response delays, largely a result of the investment that Google. Bing and services have made in web search, so even a delay of 20 seconds waiting for a set of results to be created can seem like a lifetime to a user.

Not only will the index contain a pointer to every word in every document it also will contain all the positional information and tagging about phrases. The result is that the size of an inverted index could be the same size, if not larger, than the total size of the repositories that have been indexed. However the indexes are usually compressed to the point that typically they may be around 30-50% of the size of the repositories. For search not only is it important to compress the size of the index (as this will reduce memory requirements and can speed processing) but there is also a requirement to decompress the index to present the results. As with so much of the technology of search the difference between the search products available on the market is often down to the basic processes of text processing, indexing, query processing and results delivery.

Throughout the working day new content is being indexed. How will this be included in the index? Some vendors are able to rebuild the index very quickly indeed and then switch incoming queries to the most recent version of the index. Other vendors will build a temporary index which is then searched in parallel with the main index and the result sets integrated into a single sequence. This approach can slow down the overall process of the search as the integration takes place.

One recent development in computing technology is in-memory database technology. This technology moves databases off of disks into random access memory (RAM) with very significant improvements in processing speed. The early adopters have been companies with interests in enterprise resource planning, content analytics and customer relationship management applications.

Security and ACLs

In many organizations certain information can only be seen by either specific employees, by employees in particular roles (for example HR) or by employees dealing with specific customer accounts. A search application has to be able recognize these limitations on access to avoid the confidentiality of information being compromised. Not only must a confidential document not be able to be downloaded from a search results screen but the very existence of the document has to be able to be concealed.

These authorization permissions are managed through Access Control Lists. An Access Control List (ACL) is a 2 by 2 matrix which defines which documents (or databases, videos and any other content indexed by the search application) can be accessed by each individual employee. The complexity of managing ACLs in a corporate environment with several hundred applications is difficult enough but scaling this to potentially millions of documents is an altogether more challenging requirement.

This reduces the complexity of the ACLs but assumes that the organization is quickly able to identify and change group memberships should a member of staff leave the organisation. In the time between someone being given notice to leave, even if it is at the end of the day the potential damage that could be caused in downloading confidential documents could be very significant.

Another aspect of access control in search is that there is very often considerable benefit in the user being able to restrict the search to specific collections of documents. For example they may only which to see documents in a specific language or only look at SharePoint repositories because they know that the information they are looking for will be in a SharePoint server. All this granularity of access presents substantial management challenges, especially because when users find out that there is content that they cannot gain access to but to which a colleague doing the same job in a different subsidiary does have access can lead to a difficult situation.

There are two basic approaches that can be used to manage access to information to which not all employees should have access.

Based on the authorization ACL a user is shown results only from those collections that they have permission to access. This is based on a collection management policy of putting limited access documents into specific collections. This approach has limited impact on retrieval speed but only works for those situations in which controlled documents fall into relatively few categories and therefore relatively few collections. As the number of collections increases the retrieval performance will decrease because of the amount of processing that is taking place prior to results display. This is often referred to as the early-binding approach to security management

The user carries out a search but before the results are displayed the user is asked for their authorization credentials. The search engine then filters the results to display only those for which the user has authorization. This works well for document-level security but has some major performance issues when implemented at a document level. This is because for each document the search application has to undertake a check of the document ACL and results in a substantial performance overhead. If the servers concerned are being heavily used then the search application may have to time-out the request for a result and the user will never know whether they have not seen a document on the basis of security or system performance. This is often referred to as the late-binding approach.

In theory there is a third approach in which all results are presented to the user, but there is a link to confidential information which requires a user to provide additional authentication before the content is displayed. Apart from the fact that the user is now aware of the existence of confidential information to which they may not have access users that do have access now have to provide additional authorization for each of the documents concerned, which can be a very slow process. In practice this is not an approach that has any benefits.

The secure access management challenges outlined above are complex enough but become even more difficult to manage when there is a federated search environment and the authorization processes and ACLs are not uniform across all collections and/or search applications.

From the viewpoint of the search application managing the delivery of information according to an ACL is quite straightforward, if somewhat processor intensive for very large repositories. The organization has to be able to uniquely identify employees or groups of employees, add, modify or remove identifiers at short notice and have a rigorous information security classification model for all the content to be indexed by the search engine.

One security loophole that is often overlooked is that some search applications provide users with suggested query terms as they enter a query into the search box. These may not be security-trimmed. A search for "redundancy" might come up with a suggestion for "redundancy strategy planning" even though the document cannot be accessed by the user.

Query Management

Query management also presents some challenges. In the case of indexing there is an enormous amount of information that the indexing process can use to 'understand' the nature of the information content. Users then expect to type in a single word and expect the search engine to undertake a mind meld and work out what the query is really about. The query processing stage has to be able to undertake four processes in very quick time:

- Check for obvious spelling mistakes and offer suggestions for alternate spellings

- Use stemming and lemmatization to develop a range of potential query terms
- Identify entities or phrases that may need to be clarified or expanded
- Apply some semantic analysis to gain an insight into the likely nature of the query

A good example of query management in action can be seen on the public web site of Microsoft at *http://www.microsoft.com*. Typing the word [SharePoint] will cause a drop-down list of key variants to appear, such as SharePoint 2007 and SharePoint 2010, as well as shared view. Sticking with [SharePoint] will produce a list of results which are entry-level publications on SharePoint for people who have no previous knowledge of the application. For the query [SharePoint 2010 Disaster Recovery] none of the entry-level results are anywhere to be seen as the query processor has made the assumption that anyone asking this question clearly knows about SharePoint technology.

For many years now there has been a significant amount of interest in using natural language processing (NLP and not to be confused with Neuro-linguistic programming!) for queries. The user types a sentence such as 'Find all the projects we have carried out in India with a gross margin of more than 30%'. This is a well-formed instruction but is the information that has been indexed able to provide an answer. The margin information might be held in a finance system and there is no link to the project lists held in SharePoint 2010.

As with all aspects of search technology it only matters that the particular approach to query management taken by a vendor works for the queries that your organization is going to generate. This is why it is important to undertake the user requirements analysis, come up with personas and use cases, and then work up some typical queries that can be used in the Proof of Concept tests.

Spell Checking

The quality of the spell checker behind the query box makes a significant difference to user satisfaction with the search process as time is not wasted looking for words that do not exist. A good spell checker not only spots incorrect spelling but offers suggestions, and this feature can be extended to auto-complete by presenting the user with a list of words that match the query term as it begins to be spelt out in the query box. Finding the balance between being helpful and getting in the way is not easy.

The suggestions will be made from a spelling dictionary that is generated from the index terms but it should also be possible to add in special terms that are of value to the organization. This could include key members of staff with names that are difficult to spell correctly or office locations in places like Rawalpindi, where it is easy to miss out the second 'a' in the name because it is not pronounced.

Retrieval Models

Two thousand words into the chapter and only now do we come to the process of information retrieval. There are four different approaches to managing the process of matching the query against the index and delivering a set of results. Users want relevant results and the three approaches, often referred to as 'models'.

The first of these models is Boolean retrieval. It is named after George Boole (1815-1864) who was an English mathematician with a special interest in algebraic logic, in which logical propositions could be expressed in algebraic terms. Boole's work was taken up by Claude Shannon in the late 1930s as the basis for managing telephone circuits and later the circuits in digital computers. Boolean algebra is characterized by the use of the operators AND, NOT and OR.

A query about the London 2012 Olympics could be represented as:

London AND Olympics AND 2012

If the user was interested in looking for information about both the 2012 and 1948 Olympics then they would use:

London AND Olympics AND (2012 OR 1948)

The nested logic within the parentheses is familiar to anyone who has had to created formulae in an Excel spread-sheet.

This approach was taken by all the early search applications but has the fundamental problem that the documents returned either meet or do not meet the query term. There is no room for fuzziness. Adding in more terms to try to be specific can result in relevant documents being excluded. It is not possible to rank the set of results as a list in descending order of relevance. This order is referred to as ranked list.

To overcome this problem Gerard Salton developed the vector space model in the late 1960s although did not publish the core papers on his work until the early 1970s. The mathematics of this model is very complex but in principle it enables the computation of how similar a document is to the terms in the query. Many current search applications make use of the vector space model.

The third model is based on probability theory. It has come to prominence over the last decade through the advocacy of this approach by Dr. Michael Lynch and his colleagues at Autonomy. The model is based on the work of the Reverend Thomas Bayes (1701 – 1761).

Finally there is the model described as latent semantic indexing, which was initially proposed in 1988 but was not commercially developed until the mid-1990s. A further stage of development came with probabilistic latent semantic indexing, used in the Recommind search software. Both of these are best regarded as an extension of the vector space model.

Search application vendors are usually unwilling to reveal exactly which model they are using in their products, and in any case it is not just the retrieval model but how the results are ranked that is of importance to a customer. Each has strong proponents but there is no one ideal model.

Ranking

All the technology outlined in this chapter is devoted to the objective of delivering a set of highly relevant results in response to any query that might be posted. Ideally the results should be ranked in descending order and again in an ideal world there would be quite a distinct cut off so that users could feel than after the initial 50 results there was not much point in continuing to look at more results. The technical and mathematical challenges in achieving this are immense and probably more research has been carried out on this aspect of information retrieval and search technology than any other.

There are a number of approaches to trying to give the user the documents they need on the first page of the search results. Absolute query and relative query boosting are two examples of static ranking, and are based on business rules. For a number of queries there could be one or more documents that are important to display either as the first or second result, or above the list of results. For example any search for some HR-related terms such as maternity or paternity leave will always result in the user being presented with both the global HR policy document and the HR policy for the local unit. Both may be highly relevant because a manager located in India may want to check what the rules are in Sweden. This is sometimes referred to as a 'Best Bet' or absolute query boosting.

Under relative query boosting for certain queries there could be one or more documents that a user should be made aware of, but which do niot merit being placed at the beginning of a results list. Any search on [corporate performance] might have a rule that ensures that the latest quarterly report is always in the top 20 results, or possibly a PowerPoint presentation given to investors.

Ranking by decreasing relevance is just one possible sequence. In the world of enterprise search date order can be important. A manager either wants to find out the most recent project reports listed in reverse chronological order (most recent first) or needs to find out the first time that a particular chemical was synthesized in the company's research laboratories.

Summarization

The results list will usually be presented as a title, some additional data (metadata) about the document and then a summary of the document. There are many different ways of creating these summaries, including taking highly relevant sentences from the document and reproducing the text a given number of words either side of a search term so that the term can be seen in context. This latter approach would seem to be an effective approach but in a long document (a feature of enterprises) this may just be a few sentences from a 200 page project report and may not be representative of the entire report.

Document Thumbnails

Another approach is to display an HTML thumbnail of the document with the search terms highlighted, and with the facility to step through each occurrence of the term. Again the more terms the less successful this approach becomes but it is especially useful for PowerPoint presentations when users are looking for a slide on which they remember there was an especially clever diagram that they would like to reuse. The extent to which thumbnails can be generated will depend on the file format of the document. Currently FAST Search Server for SharePoint 2010 can only do so with Microsoft Office documents.

Another benefit of using document thumbnails is that it avoids the need to open up the document in another application just to view it for long enough to determine that the document is not relevant and close it down again. That puts quite a load on the hardware and network bandwidth. The quality of the thumbnails varies as far as being an accurate representation of the document.

Summary

The technology described in this Chapter is the base technology for all search applications. Each vendor, or open-source application, will have their own approach to exactly how each of these processes is delivered but trying to differentiate between them on the basis of these core processes is not a good use of time. As with any software application it is not how a process is carried out but whether the results are of value to the organization.

Further Reading

Many of the books listed in Appendix A cover the mathematics and technology of search in very considerable detail. However none of them provide any specific information on the technology suites used by individual search vendors.

CHAPTER 6

Search Technology Part 2

In this chapter some of the more sophisticated aspects of search technology are described. All search applications will have the technology components described in Chapter 5 but few will have all the technologies set out in this chapter. In selecting a search application it is of little value to use this chapter as a check-list, making a short list from those applications having the greatest number of ticks.

The reasons for this are:

- Selecting a search application has to be based on user requirements, and it could be that just one of these features correctly implemented will be quite sufficient to meet these requirements.

- The more of these features that are implemented the greater the cost of implementation and administration, ease of upgrading may be reduced, and users may need more training and support.

Entity Extraction

The concept of entity extraction is to be able to use the search application to identify automatically personal names, locations and other terms that can then be used as query terms without the need to manually index these terms. The technical term for this process is 'named entity extraction' and analyses not just an individual word but also a sequence of words to determine index terms that could be of value in responding to queries. When organizations choose English they are also choosing a language with over 1,000,000 words, a result of invasions and the scale of perhaps the British Empire. The result is a language full of synonyms and polysemes. Fortunately words do not appear in isolation (other than in tables and charts!) so an analysis of a sentence will help substantially in determining the meaning of a word. The mathematics of entity extraction is largely based on the mathematics of Markov Models. A Markov Model describes a process as a collection of states and transitions between states, each of which can be given a probability. Although a knowledge of Markov Models, Hidden Markov Models and the Viterbi algorithm are not a requirement for a search support team it does illustrate the extent to which search is based on mathematics. These and many related mathematical models will be used in different ways by each search vendor and will lead to subtle differences in search performance. These can only be assessed through careful testing at a Proof of Concept stage.

A list of some of the typical entities that can be extracted is given below:

- Credit card number
- Currency
- Date
- Distance
- Email
- Location
- Longitude/Latitude
- Nationality
- Number
- Organization
- Person
- Phone number
- Post Code
- Time
- URL

This extraction can be accomplished in four different ways, though many search applications will use all three in a blended approach:

- Statistical models provide a means of recognizing never-seen-before names and providing good answers when words can have multiple meanings. Analyzing the correlation with the other words helps identify the correct context such as deciding when the word "Paris" is used as the name of a person or a city.
- Telephone numbers and credit cards have standard formats, so as these are indexed a set of rules can be used to determine the category of the entity. This could be extended to other entities such as part numbers. For bd436678 all that is needed is to be able to write a rule that any character string starting with bd and a six digit number is a part number.

- Dictionaries and gazetteers will support the extraction of places and groups of places, so that a search for EU will also offer a search for all the Member States of the European Union.
- Specific terms can be defined by the organization.

In the case of the part number example it may well be advisable to allow for variations such as BD 436678, BD-436678, #BD436678 and even 436678BD.

People Search

A particularly important aspect of entity extraction is in searching for people in an organisation, either by name or by expertise. The reason for going into this level of detail on people search is that this is one of the most important uses of search applications, and is also one of easiest for a user to evaluate. All they have to do is search for someone they know. From the moment they find that the search application does not find this person they are unlikely to trust the search engine again.

The majority of name matching variations that occur within a language and across languages have been categorized by Basis Technologies, and the text of this section is based on a Basis Technologies white paper "The Name Matching You Need – A Comparison of Name Matching Technologies".

Typographical errors
   A slip of the finger at the keyboard causes transposition on of characters, missed characters or other similar errors. (e.g., "Htomas" or "Elizbeth").

Phonetic spelling variations
   Some names simply sound alike, but are spelled differently (e.g. "Christian" and "Kristian").

   Neglecting to confirm spelling produces errors. (e.g., "Cairns" vs. "Kearns" vs. "Kerns"; or "Smith" vs. "Smyth").

Transliteration spelling differences
   Multiple transliteration standards or "approximate" transliterations from a non-Latin script to English lead to multiple spelling variations. In the case of Arabic to English, Arabic has many consonant sounds which might be written with the same English letter, or Arabic vowels may be expressed more than one way in English, giving rise tomany spelling variations. (e.g., "Abdul Rasheed" vs. "Abd-al-Rasheed" vs. "Abd Ar-Rashid").

Initials
   Sometimes all name components are spelled out, other times initials are used. (e.g., "Mary A. Hall" vs. " Mary Alice Hall" vs. "M.A. Hall").

Nicknames

In some cultures, nicknames are numerous and may be often used in place of a person's formal name (e.g., "Elizabeth", "Beth", "Liz", and "Lisbeth").

Re-ordered name components

The order of family name and given name may appear swapped due to database format or ignorance of cultural naming convention. (e.g., "JohnHenry" vs. "Henry, John"; or "Tanaka Kentaro" vs. "Kentaro Tanaka").

Missing name components

Sometimes a middle name or patronymic (personal name derived from ancestor's name—e.g., Olafsson = "son of Olaf") may be absent. (e.g., "Abdullah Al-Ashqar" vs. " Abdullah Bin Hassan Al-Ashqar"; or "Philip Charles Carr" vs. "Philip Carr".

Missing spaces

Some names are commonly written with spaces in different places, bothin common English names (e.g., "Mary Ellen", "Maryellen", and "Mary-Ellen") and those less-common in English (e.g., "Zhang Jing Quan" and "Zhang Jingquan").

Names in different languages

Names from languages using different writing systems can be notoriously diffcult to match against English representations of the names. Here is just onename spelled in English, Russian, simplified Chinese, and traditional Chinese, respectively:

Common key

These methods, such as Soundex, reduce names to a key or code based on their English pronunciation, such that similar sounding names share the same key. Common key methods are fast and produce high recall (finds most of the correct answers) but have generally ow precision (i.e., contain many false hits). Precision is yet lower when matching non-Latin script names, which first must be transliterated to Latin characters to use this method.

List-method

This method attempts to list all possible spelling variations of each namecomponent and then uses the name variation lists to look for matches against the target name. The result can be slow performance if very large lists must be searched. Furthermore, thismethod will not match name variations not appearing in its lists.

Edit distance

This approach looks at edit distance, that is, how many character changes it takes to get from one name to another. For example, "Catherine" and "Katherine" have an editdistance of 1 since the "C" is substituted for "K." Edit distance methods work for Latin-to-Latin name comparisons, but precision suffers as each edit is weighted similarly, so a replacement of"c" for "k" is considered equal to a replacement of "z" for "t."

Statistical similarity

A statistical approach trains a model to recognize what two "similar names" look like so that the model can take two names and assign a probability that the two names match or not. This method produces high precision results, but may be slower than the common key method.

It is easy to take the position that, because the organization does not operate in Chinese or Arabic languages, there is no potential problem with people search. This is very unlikely to be the case even for an organisation working in a single country. The capability of a search application to deal with the name variants highlighted above should be a core element of the Proof of Concept tests. (See Chapter 8)

Federated Search

In most enterprise applications information resides in many different repositories, ranging from a public drive to a sophisticated document management system. One of the mantras of enterprise search is that the user should not need to know where information is stored in order to be able to find it. However subsequently knowing where an item of information has been stored may help the user assess the value of the information. Documents are usually only added to a document or records management application when there are good and defined business reasons for doing so.

There are two different approaches to federated search:

An index can be built of all the content in each repository. When a search is carried out the source of a document is tagged with its location so that a) the user can select which repositories are searched and b) if more than one repository is being searched the user can identify the source from the information about each search result. In theory this would be the ideal approach but in reality the size of the index and the computing power needed to search it can be significant.

A repository may have its own search application, perhaps embedded within a document management system. The search query box sends the search to each of these individual search applications, which then generates a set of results. A complete set of results is then presented to the user.

Federated search gives rise to a substantial issue in relevance ranking. A search carried out on the native search in SharePoint is quite likely to present the user with a ranking list that bears no relation to the same search carried out on the same SharePoint repository using (as an example) Autonomy as a cross-enterprise search application. In principle it is a very valuable approach but in practice it can be a nightmare to achieve useful outcomes on a predictable basis.

What ever a vendor promises as a federated search solution it is of the greatest importance that the solution is tested rigorously during a Proof of Concept evaluation, paying particular attention to the user interface and how the user will then refine their intial query.

Duplicate and Similar Documents

It is not unusual to find that at the end of a Google search where there have been relatively few results presented a comment from the search engine that the results presented have excluded duplicated documents, which can be viewed if the user requests. In an enterprise situation duplicate documents are quite common. For a start there could be multiple versions of the same document, or the same version (perhaps an internal memorandum or corporate policy) has been posted by most, if not all, of the business units in an organization.

Exact matches, such as an internal memorandum, can be identified through creating a 'checksum' of the bytes in the document, which can be extended through use of cyclic redundancy checking. Things get much more difficult with near-duplicates. To take the example of an internal memorandum there could be versions in different languages (and therefore different checksums) or where the memorandum has been published with a different date, a different title or a summary in more than one language. There are a number of solutions to finding near-duplicates, the mathematics of which fall outside the scope of this book.

Finding similar documents seems at first sight to be the converse of de-duplication, but in practice just want is meant by a 'similar document'. If the corporate HR policy has been found as the result of a search would the corporate risk policy be a similar document, or perhaps business unit HR policies. The question also needs to be asked about why the search application has delivered a set of relevant documents there should be other similar documents that have not been presented. Sometimes the answer is that the 'similar to' only applies to documents in the set of results and is a way of providing the user with a more precise set of results. The technology approach is also very different, because the search application will be looking at all the index information on a set of documents, not just on the length of the document.

Mobile Search

Mobile search is about to present some significant challenges to the search community. Over the last few years search results pages have become cluttered with filters and facets. Presenting all this information onto a tablet device or onto a smartphone is not going to be easy. On a pc the control device will be through a full-size keyboard and a mouse, supported by a printer. The user of a smartphone will expect to be able to use voice commands, a finger and or a swipe, and be able to save results for printing out at a later time. In addition there will be an expectation that the search will be context sensitive, so that if the user is in France the results presented may be different from those carried out in Australia.

It is now certain that there will be wide-scale use of tablets and smartphones to access enterprise information, not just from employees working outside the office but also from employees working in large distributed office campus sites, such as a university. The devices used may be the personal property of the employee (Bring Your Own Device) and so authentication may be a major problem.

The rate of adoption of smartphones and in particular tablets seems to have caught the search industry by surprise. Isys-Search was one of the early leaders in developing mobile-specific user interfaces and only gradually are other vendors beginning to offer similar capabilities.

Faceted Search

Faceted search is a good example of where information science meets information retrieval. The most familiar use of faceted search is on e-commerce sites where it is possible to sequentially add terms to a query to drill down into what was originally a large results set. The starting point on a used car web site could have been [Ford] giving 1232 cars for sale. Using the search interface it will then be possible to look for Ford cars with a price between $5000 and $12000, reducing the options to 340. Adding the colour [black] might bring the total down to 34, at which point browsing takes over. This search could also have been conducted using a parametric search in which each of these values is selected from a set of drop-down lists, in effect constructing a long Boolean expression. The downside is that if there are no black Ford cars priced between $5000 and $12000 then the results set is zero and the user has to start all over again. Most 'advanced search' options work the same way, and can give the same end result.

The concept of faceted search dates back to the work of the Indian mathematician and librarian S.R. Ranganathan. He developed an alternative to the hierarchical approach adopted by library classification schemes such as the Dewey Decimal Classification (DDC). He named his approach as the colon classification scheme because in describing a document each element was separated by a colon:

Car:Ford:$6000:black

Ranganathan described these facets as 'isolates' each of which could have its own hierarchy. The information science of facets is described and their value in search is well by both Daniel Tunkelang and Marti Hearst.

To focus on their role in enterprise search, most search vendors now offer a range of facets on the user interface. These might include 'date' and 'file type'. The ability to reduce a set of results by date is very useful in enterprise search, and indeed is a feature of Google web search. The problem is that 'date' is a very challenging parameter and could be (for example):

- The date the document was first released.
- The date that the latest amendment was made to the document.
- The date that the server on which the document is stored was last re-installed.

When it comes to 'file type' then being able to select PowerPoint files related to the search could be very useful. Being offered the choice between HTML, Word and pdf files pre-supposes that these file types indicate a value ranking on a document, which is almost certainly not the case.

Another option is to use the indexing capability of the search engine to provide a facet based on auto-categorisation and entity extraction. A search for [sea water corrosion] would then generate a list of all employees that had either written reports on sea water corrosion, been a member of a project team on sea water corrosion or been referred to a customer visit report. It might also be used to create a set of all components which had been tested for their resistance to sea water corrosion.

In his book Daniel Tunkelang makes the following important observation:

> As it turns out, faceted search is much like chess – it takes only minutes to grasp the rules but years to get to grips with playing the game well.

When assessing the faceted search offerings of a vendor, or designing them in to an open-source application the following issues should be considered:

- Given the breadth of content how many different facets could be of value to the user?
- Will all these facets be presented in the same user interface or will only a sub-set of facets be presented based on the query?
- How easy is it (if indeed possible at all) for the search support team to create new facets and remove or modify facets that are not being used to refine a set of search results?
- What is the mobile device experience going to be with the facets that work well on a large screen desk-top monitor?
- Will the search logs pick up which terms have been selected from each of the facets?

- Will the sum of the number of occurrences of each element in each facet be roughly the same as the total set size?

The reason for the last of these issues is that if for example the sum of all the occurrences by date sums to 650 and yet the total number of results presented is 1340 the user is going to be concerned about the discrepancy and wonder if the search application is working correctly. The reason for this is usually because the search application is using a predictive count based on the first (say) 100 results. Other applications may be doing a count on all occurrences. Just one more thing to check at Proof of Concept stage!

Multilingual Search

Despite the attempts by international companies to make English the corporate language in reality there will be content in multiple languages. Just as English and American English have variations in meaning (petrol and gas) the same is the case in other apparently similar languages. European Portuguese and Brazilian Portuguese is just one example. A railway train is 'comboio' in the former and 'trem' in the latter.

The initial challenge for a search engine is to recognise the language and then undertake all the linguistic analysis needed to index the documents. There are then two options. Usually the user has to enter search terms in all the appropriate languages, either in sequential searches or using an OR command in an advanced search box. Alternatively a thesarus could be used to generate Brazilian search terms. This means that the user does not have to know that the words are different in the two languages.

Search-Based Applications

The concept of search-based applications is just as difficult to define as Big Data and Unified Information Access. Sue Feldman at International Data Corporation offers probably the best description:

- They are built on a search backbone to enable fast access to information in multiple formats.
- Are designed as a unified work environment to support a specific task or workflow, for example, e-discovery, fraud detection, voice of the customer, sales prospecting, research, or customer support.
- Integrate all the tools that are commonly needed for that task including information access, authoring, reporting and analysis and information visualization.
- Unify access to multiple repositories of information in multiple formats.

- Integrate domain knowledge to support the particular task, including industry taxonomies and vocabularies, internal processes, workflow for the task, connectors to collections of information.

Another way of looking at these applications is that it is search without a search query box. The queries are created from the working processes of the user. One simple example is the Rightmove house agency (*http://www.rightmove.co.uk.*) in the UK which offers users the ability to draw a complex polygon to define the area in which they are looking for a house.

What these applications take advantage of, and the same is true of unified information access, is that the technology that has been developed over many years to handle unstructured content is equally adept at not only searching structured databases but then integrating the information from both source categories at very high levels of performance.

Semantic Search

Semantic search is a very broad term used by many search vendors to promote the ability of their software to semantically comprehend language. Sematic analysis should enable a user to look for examples of 'new product development' and find information relating to the concept without any of the three words appearing anywhere in the document.

There is an immense amount of research and application development being undertaken into semantic search. Evaluting the semantic search capabilities of search applications cannot be undertaken in any way other than through Proof of Concept tests.

Social Search

There is a rapidly increasing amount of 'user generated content' in organizations with the adoption of social media applications. This content, if indexed and searched, could provide valuable information about the knowledge and networks of employees. There are two challenges. First this content may use social phrases and acronyms and also make the assumption that readers will have the context to understand the content. "Are you going to John's meeting this afternoon? There is likely to be battle over the ownership of the project!" makes the assumption that the recipient knows who John is, where the meeting is going to be held and what project is going to be discussed.

Second it is difficult to decide what weight to give this content in an overall list of results. In some respects it may be of great value, especially to people in the meeting, but to others it has no value at all.

Another aspect of social search is offering users the option to be able to tag search results with a rating of the value of the content or adding a comment on the document. In principle this seems to be a very useful feature but in practice the challenge is how much weight to put on these personal comments. As with any review it does not matter what the notional credibility of the person who has added the tags is, but the credibility of this person from the viewpoint of the potential user of the information.

Text Mining and Sentiment Analysis

Text mining is sometimes regarded as a synonym for search, but that is not the case. Text mining seeks to identify the occurrence of clusters of related terms in a collection of documents, and then present an analysis of these over a period of time. For example a collection of call-centre transcripts could be mined to see the relationship between certain products and the types of complaints expressed by users. A hair-drier may be described as 'heavy', 'awkward' or 'difficult to use'. A text mining application will try to build clusters of related terms, often presenting them graphically for further analysis.

A related area is that of sentiment analysis, perhaps looking to see if over a period of time following a modification of the hair-dryer customers seem to be satisfied with its performance.

Summary

The range of features now offered by search applications is very wide indeed and will continue to increase. It is easy to work on the basis that the more features the better the search application but this may not be the case. The variations in performance of all the features outlined in this chapter need to be assessed against the content to be searched and the way in which users will search this content. If name entity extraction would be of value then the search applications need to be tested against the corporate HR database and not assessed on the basis of a description in a brochure or a demonstration by the vendor.

Further Reading

You'll find some additional information regarding the subject matter of this chapter in the "Further Reading" (page 156) section in Appendix A.

CHAPTER 7

The Business of Search

Compared to most sectors of the enterprise applications business the enterprise search business is quite small. The total annual sales of search software may only amount to $3billion at most, which in IT terms is a niche market. In total there are probably no more than 80 companies in the business at present, and these are listed in Appendix B. It is very likely that business and IT managers will not be aware of any of these companies with the possible exception of Google. Most of them have revenues of less than $50million and many may have revenues of less than $10million. However this figure excludes the revenues of the search modules in large enterprise suites from IBM, Oracle, SAP and Microsoft, as well as sales of Google search appliances.

Another way of looking at the search market is the installed base of enterprise search. Excluding the enterprise suite market probably only Ultraseek (acquired by Autonomy when it purchased Verity), Isys-Search and Google have reached the 10,000 installed base mark, but the majority of these implementations are relatively small-scale.

The good news is that if the installed base is small then the potential is significant. One of the side effects of the acquisition of Autonomy, Endeca and Isys-Search in 2011/2012 was that current and potential investors can see a trade sale of a search vendor as an exit strategy to gain a return on their investment. It does not take much to set up a search software business. It is mainly about brain power. Designers of search software need to have skills in the mathematics of probability, computational linguistics and database design. Previous experience in search development is useful but by no means essential as the mathematics of search uses well-established mathematical principles. Many specialized modules, such as document filters and language parsers, can be bought in. One of the outcomes of the search acquisition frenzy in 2011/2012 is that talented search developers may wish to pursue their career outside of a large IT company.

In this chapter an outline is given of the enterprise search business. In the period from mid-2011 to mid-2012 four significant acquisitions have changed the business landscape and the implications of these acquisitions are important to understand when considering potential suppliers of search software.

Industry Structure

There are three categories of search vendors. The first of these consists of a small number of large IT companies who offer their customers enterprise search software but often bundled into large enterprise suites.

Dassault

Dassault, the French enterprise systems company, acquired Exalead in 2010. Exalead had development both a public web search service and a powerful enterprise search application that was one of the first to be available as a cloud-based application. Exalead has also been a leader in the development of search-based applications and solutions for 'big data' applications.

HP

HP acquired Autonomy in 2011 for around $8billion. Autonomy was UK-based company and was the only search vendor to be publicly listed. The company did much to raise the profile of enterprise search around the world. However the fit between an entrepreneurial company of 2000 employees and HP with over 350,000 employees was always going to be a difficult one to engineer. By mid-2012 many senior Autonomy managers had left the company and contract with Dr. Mike Lynch, the founder of Autonomy, was terminated.

IBM

IBM has a long history of research and development in information retrieval. Over the years it has acquired many small companies with search expertise, rapidly integrating them into its core product range. IBM's Omnifind search product is based on the Apache-Lucene open-source search application. In 2012 IBM acquired Vivisimo, a search application developed at the Carniege-Mellon University.

Lexmark

Lexmark was founded in 1991 when IBM divested its printer business. In 2012 it diversified into the search business acquiring Brainware and then Isys-Search. Isys-Search, an Australian-based company, was a leading vendor of midrange enterprise search applications. Lexmark had previously acquired Perceptive Software in 2011, a supplier of enterprise content management and business process management software. Although Isys-Search was a very visible acquisition it is likely that Brainware may emerge as the flagship product. Brainware claims to have invested over $100 million in research and development.

Oracle

Oracle has been in the search business for many years, launching Oracle Secure Search in 2006. Unlike IBM Oracle has been more than happy to sell the product to non-Oracle customers. In 2011, probably in a reaction to the HP acquisition of Autonomy, Oracle acquired Endeca, a search vendor that specialized in filtering search results for applications such as e-commerce sites. Oracle moved quickly to integrate Endeca into its product catalogue.

With all these companies there are some trade-offs between benefits and risks when choosing their search solutions. The benefits are that these companies have the financial resources, sales teams and commercial incentives to ensure that the costs of acquisition are defrayed as soon as possible. They will almost certainly have existing contracts with major companies and will quickly be in a position to offer enhanced search applications. Procurement departments will feel comfortable that the companies will remain in existence for some years to come, and IT managers know that they will be able to call on service and support teams in most countries of the world.

There are also risks to be considered. Search is such a small element of total sales the sales teams will probably not have the detailed product knowledge that is essential in ensuring that user requirements can be met by the vendor's search solutions. In the case of IBM and Oracle, and to a lesser extent Lexmark, the companies have multiple search applications to offer. Organizations who have already implemented Autonomy, Isys-Search, Endeca, and Vivisimo will find that the people they have been dealing with for some time may not have the same degree of commitment to the product or are not able to make commitments to solving problems with the same degree of rapidity as they have done in the past.

Independent Search Vendors

There are probably around 70 independent search vendors whose main line of business is the development of search applications. They are mostly funded by venture capital and private equity placements. Because of their small size there are no requirements to publish detailed accounts of corporate revenues. Most of these independent search vendors have revenues of less than $20 million, and many operate largely in a specific national market to reduce the costs of customer sales and support. Indeed one of the outcomes of the search acquisition frenzy in 2011/2012 was that the mid-market search industry, with revenues of $50M to $150M, virtually disappeared.

The challenge that these companies face is that they cannot afford to do much in the way of marketing and are virtually unknown to most IT managers. There is also a procurement issue in that procurement departments are always concerned about potential suppliers that have no published accounts. All the vendors will provide financial information under a non-disclosure agreement but in many cases the profits will be minimal as they are being ploughed back into the development of the software. Even then the number of people who have a full understanding of the search software code base will be quite small.

Open Source Search Software

The development of open source software dates back to the early 1980s and the launch of the GNU Project by Richard Stallman at MIT and some small-scale open source search applications were developed in the 1990s, mainly for web site search. In 1999 Doug Cutting released Lucene as a SourceForge project and donated the code to the Apache Foundation in 2001. Around the same time Yonik Seely developed the Solr application for CNET and then donated the code to the Apache Foundation in 2006.

In December 2004, Google Labs published a paper on the MapReduce algorithm, which allows very large scale computations to be run in parallel across large clusters of servers. Cutting, at that time working for Yahoo!, took the concepts in the MapReduce algorithm and created the open-source Hadoop framework that allows applications based on the MapReduce algorithm to be implemented on large server clusters.

Although there is now a high level of awareness of Apache Lucence/Solr as an open source enterprise search application there are a number of others, notably Xapian. This is based on the Muscat search application written by Dr. Martin Porter at the University of Cambridge in 1984. ElasticSearch is interesting as the company that supports the software received a $10M investment in late 2012.

Open-source applications often require the integration of modules from other sources to meet particular user requirements, and are certainly not out-of-the box applications which can be implemented without expertise not only in (usually) Java programming but also in the basic principles of information retrieval and enterprise search optimization.

One of terms often used in the open-source community is that of someone being a 'committer'. Committers are either project founders, developers appointed by the project founders, or voted into the role by the community. They are responsible for writing the majority of code for a project as well as for the review of patches submitted by the community.

There are three business/implementation models:

- An organization can download the software code and use internal developers

- Use a company with expertise in the development of the selected open source application

- Implement a 'productized' version of the open source application, for example from Lucidworks.

LucidWorks currently employs about 25% of the committers to the Apache Lucene/Solr project, making it probably the largest supplier of productized open source solutions. It has strategic partnerships with around 30 implementation partners around the world.

The open source enterprise search business is going to develop substantially over the next few years. The spate of acquisitions in 2011 and 2012 and the question marks over the future of FAST ESP have both caused organizations (other than maybe those implementing SharePoint) to look more carefully at the potential benefits of a customized open-source development option. One of the justifications that often cited for open source search software is that it enables the organization to escape being tied in to a single vendor. The Apache Lucene/Solr stack is fast becoming the de facto open-source search software, supported by a very vigorous global community. In principle there is no license-fee/proprietary code lock-in but in reality the challenges of changing from Lucene-Solr to another open-source solution should not be underestimated.

Although there is a substantial community supporting Apache Lucene and Solr in particular that does not mean that the community will provide a virtual support team for the implementation and management of open-source search applications. Implementation support will be provided by companies such as LucidWorks, Intrafind and Polyspot who have built search applications on top of Lucene and Solr. The rule is that you get what you pay for.

It is also important to note that Java is not open-source but is owned and developed by Oracle. In 2011 changes made to Java by Oracle caused some problems for the open-source search community. Lessons were learned and it is unlikely to happen again.

Google and Search Appliances

A search appliance is a search application and disk storage ready installed in a standard rack casing. In principle it can be installed and switched on in perhaps 30 minutes. The product concept has been made famous by Google with its Enterprise Search Appliance, but Google was not the first company to offer an appliance product. The search appliance was pioneered by the US company Thunderstone in 2003, though the company itself was founded in 1981.

The Google innovation was the pricing policy, which is based on the number of documents to be indexed and searched. The search-appliance license points begin at indexing 500,000 documents, and extend all the way up to 30 million documents or more. The Google Search Appliance is offered at two- or three-year license points, which include support, hardware replacement coverage, and software updates. When the contract period ends a new contract has to be negotiated. It is important to remember that customer support from Google is very limited indeed. Email is the standard communications channel and finding the name of someone in Google with whom a dialogue can be established is almost certainly going to be impossible.

This means that some careful calculations have to be made about the total cost of ownership over a five year period that would be the minimum typical life-span for a more conventional application. Most companies have no idea of how much information they need to index, much less the number of documents. Multiple versions of the same document quickly increase the number being indexed. Another factor to be considered is the cost of purchasing additional server licenses to provide for redundancy in the event of a server failure and also for development and test purposes.

In general search appliances offer very good processing performance because the software and hardware are fully integrated by the vendor. However it is usually difficult to tune appliances to improve relevancy, the range of connectors to other applications is limited and customer support is often restricted to a local partner.

Over the last few years the number of search appliances has increased and shortly after the acquisition of Autonomy by HP an appliance version of the Autonomy search software was announced. MaxxCAT, Perfect Search and Fabasoft Mindbreeze are three other search appliance vendors.

In mid-2012 Google withdrew its Google Mini appliance from the market. The enterprise appliances are still being sold and supported but as always with Google a decision could be made with little warning to withdraw from the market. With total revenues in 2011 of around $38 billion the enterprise search business is probably worth 0.01% of these revenues.

Microsoft SharePoint

Microsoft came late to enterprise search. The search functionality of the 2007 release of SharePoint was poor and in an effort to catch up Microsoft acquired the Norwegian software company FAST Search and Transfer in 2008. FAST ESP was a very powerful enterprise search application running on Linux servers. Microsoft moved the application to Windows servers and used the expertise of the company's developers to enhance the search functionality of SharePoint 2010.

The range of search applications available from Microsoft is quite complicated to understand:

- Search Server Express is a free product that can be downloaded from Microsoft and installed on a single server. It can be used to index up to 300,000 items.

- Search Server 2010 has the same functionality as Search Server Express but can index up to 10 million items per server, and up to 100 million items on multiple servers. There is a per-server license fee.

- SharePoint Server 2010 is the entry-level search for SharePoint 2010. It is bundled in to the Standard CAL (Client Access License).

- FAST Search Server 2010 for SharePoint brings much (but certainly not all) of the functionality of FAST ESP to SharePoint search. The power and complexity of the product are both substantially greater than SharePoint Server 2010.

- FAST ESP is one of the most powerful search applications on the market, but has not been developed in any way since it was purchased by Microsoft in 2008. It goes out of main-stream support in July 2013. There is no upgrade path from FAST Search Server 2010.

Many organizations are confused by the FAST prefix to FAST Search Server for Share-Point 2010 and think that they have purchased the FAST ESP product. That is not the case. Certainly FAST Search Server for SharePoint 2010 (FS4SP) provides considerable search functionality but it is configured to run inside SharePoint. As a result the processing power and ability to customize the application are somewhat reduced. The features of FAST Search Server fall into four categories when compared to those in Share-Point Search Server:

- Features common to both products
- Features are in principle common to both products but which are enhanced in FAST Search Server
- Features are unique to FAST Search Server
- Features are unique to SharePoint Search Server

Outside of larger multi-national implementations the administration and tuning of SharePoint Search Server for SharePoint 2010 can probably be accomplished without a full-time search support team. That is not the case for FAST Search Server 2010 if the organization wants to gain the full return on the additional investment.

SharePoint 2010 was released in May 2010 and in July 2012 details started to emerge of changes to the search in SharePoint 2013. It seems likely that FS4SP will have enhanced functionality and will also be used in Exchange Server. Although some elements of the administration of FS4SP will be improved this will remain a complex application to manage. It is optimized for SharePoint implementations and using it as the basis for a large-scale enterprise search implementation needs to be considered very carefully indeed. It is important to appreciate that when implementing FS4SP there will almost certainly need to be a significant investment in server hardware over and above the CAL and related software licenses.

The search functionality of SharePoint 2007 (often referred to as MOSS07) was poor and many organizations used on of the many third-party solutions (such as those from BA-Insight, Coveo and Surfray) that were designed specifically for SharePoint. As a result few Microsoft Partners developed any expertise in search implementation, and had to build this capability with the arrival of SharePoint 2010. Even now the skills needed to implement FAST Search Server for SharePoint 2010 are in short supply and this should be taken into account when looking at the development path for search within a SharePoint environment.

Specialized Search Components

Some of the software modules used in enterprise search applications are highly specialized. This is particularly the case with the management of languages. Two companies, Basis Technology and Teragram, are the market leaders in providing very sophisticated text analytics applications. Both companies have developed techniques for parsing and indexing Arabic and Asian languages that are widely used within the search industry. Another important sector is the development of document filters.

Cloud-Based Search

Another important development is the availability of cloud-based search-as-a-service applications. Hosted search services have been used for web sites for well over a decade but have failed to make any inroads into the enterprise sector because of concerns over security management, data protection (from companies in the EU) and customisation to meet specific requirements. Over the last year a number of companies have started to highlight the benefits of using cloud-based search services, mainly in terms of getting something started and then being able to accommodate growth without the need to switch vendor to do so.

During 2012 there were a number of important announcements from Amazon (Cloud-Search) and Microsoft Azure. Search Technologies, a major search systems integrator, has set up a demonstration of Amazon CloudSearch using Wikipedia as the content source. Autonomy has a large private cloud service, which was probably one reason for its acquisition by HP in 2011.

This business model makes the costs of implementing search much more transparent than is the case with either commercial vendors (who never release even indicative license feeds) and open source developers.

There have been some negative comments about cloud-based search, many about the lack of security and the need to upload documents. These comments fail to take into account that cloud-based search, and indeed other cloud-based applications, are still in their infancy. There can be little doubt that the functionality of these search services will continue to grow, and it would not be surprising to see Google make some significant move into cloud-based search delivery in the near future.

OEM Applications

Some vendors will provide a version of their search application to companies in the document management, customer relationship management and other enterprise applications.. The version supplied to the customer may well have a reduced functionality compared to the current version of the product, and indeed may not be subject to the same upgrade roadmap as the stand-alone search product. In addition it is highly unlikely that the search application can be extended to search other repositories.

Systems Integrators

Smaller search vendors will often work directly with clients, especially where the software has been designed to work out-of-the-box. There may be a need for two-three days of support, mainly around the installation of the software on the server, sorting out disaster recovery options and testing them, and setting up the crawl routines.

There are now a number of systems integration companies that specialize in search implementation projects, offering a range of services including defining the search requirements, managing the process of product selection and then supporting the implementation. Most of these companies tend to focus their business around a selection of search software applications, but will have the skills and expertise to handle almost any search implementation project.

In some cases the vendor itself may feel that the implementation process is too complex for them to support, especially in countries where they may have little or no local office support, or where there are particular technical issues to be overcome, and will then partner with a local search systems integrator. This is usually a win-win situation for all concerned, though it is wise to make sure that integration team is fully conversant with the version of the search software they are planning to implement.

Often a company has outsourced its IT services, or uses a systems integrator to provide support for the implementation of new applications. Search implementation usually only represents a very small revenue opportunity for systems integrators, and so there may not be many staff who can manage a search implementation. For this reason systems integrators work with a small number of search vendors who can provide back-up support to their consultants. It is therefore not surprising that a search integrator only works with a small number of search vendors.

e-Discovery

e-Discovery applications are used to identify information that is required to be produced in a court case. This is a specialized area of information retrieval and with the exception of Autonomy, IBM and Recommind the vendors in this sector are focused on e-discovery processes. This is a market that has largely been driven by the compliance requirements of the U.S. Federal Rules on Civil Procedure that were first released in 2006. The industry has developed the Electronic Discovery Reference Model as a means of evaluating vendor applications.

Information Management
Managing assets in order to mitigate risk and expense should e-discovery become an issue, from initial creation of electronically stored information (ESI) through its final disposition.

Identification
Locating potential sources of ESI and determining its scope, breadth & depth.

Preservation
Ensuring that ESI is protected against inappropriate alteration or destruction.

Collection
Gathering ESI for further use in the e-discovery process (processing, review, etc.).

Processing
Reducing the volume of ESI and converting it, if necessary, to forms more suitable for review and analysis.

Review
Evaluating ESI for relevance and privilege.

Analysis
Evaluating ESI for content and context, including key patterns, topics, people and discussion.

Production
Delivering ESI to others in appropriate forms & using appropriate delivery mechanisms.

Presentation
Displaying ESI before audiences (at depositions, hearings, trials, etc.), especially in native and near-native forms, to elicit further information, validate existing facts or positions, or persuade an audience.

Summary

The range of options now available to an organization wishing to upgrade its search application is very wide indeed. It will probably not be until later in 2013 that the integration of Autonomy, Endeca, Vivisimo and Isys-Search will have been completed, and in mid-2013 Microsoft will be rolling out the next version of SharePoint with an upgraded FS4SP application. Cloud services will continue to develop and there will be increasing uptake of open-source search solutions. Meanwhile, as described in Chapter 11, the search business is changed from just focusing on text search to providing some form of unified information access capability and there will certainly be rapid development of mobile search applications.

Further Reading

You'll find some additional information regarding the subject matter of this chapter in the "Further Reading" (page 156) section in Appendix A.

CHAPTER 8

Specification and Selection

Now that all the work has been done on identifying user requirements and reviewing the performance of the current search application perhaps the time has arrived to specify, select and install a new enterprise search application. In many respects the processes for selecting an enterprise search application is just the same as for other enterprise applications but there are some differences.

These include:

- The company will not have undertaken the procurement of an enterprise search application before so there is no prior experience to go on.

- Even if there are existing search applications the level of knowledge inside the IT department about how they work and how to evaluate an enterprise application is likely to be low.

- There is probably no single business owner of search and yet it is because of the poor performance of existing search applications that the company is now undertaking the selection of a new application.

- Most of the companies in the business are totally unknown to either the IT department or to procurement.

- It is not easy for a company to understand the differences between the applications offered by the vendors and by open-source developers

- If the procurement doesn't deliver significantly better search performance the failure will be immediately apparent to most employees on the day it is launched.

This chapter provides advice on how to undertake the specification and selection of an enterprise search application.

The Project Teams

Surely it should be 'project team'? Not for an enterprise search application. There are three projects and a programme to be considered:

- The project to write the specification for the enterprise search application
- The project to select the vendor and/or integrator/developer
- The project to install the application
- The programme to manage the implementation

It is far too easy to see the enterprise search project as coming to a halt when the software is installed. One of the key messages of this book is that the hard work really starts once the software has been installed.

This chapter covers the management of the projects for writing the specification and selecting the vendor. Chapter 9 covers the installation and initial implementation and Chapter 10 provides advice on the on-going management of the application.

It is advisable to work out who is going to be on the three project teams and the search support team (see Chapter 10) right at the outset of the entire project. It may be that there are some gaps for which currently there are not people with the appropriate skills and experience, or perhaps the time to work on the project. These will need to be identified and filled ahead of the appropriate stage of the project. The gap that cannot exist is that of the Search Manager, the person who will ultimately have the responsibility for making sure that the search application meets the needs of the business and every individual employee who uses it. This position is so important that if a Search Manager cannot be identified and appointed then it would be advisable to delay the start of even writing the specification until the position is filled. The blend of skills in the three project teams will be different but the common factor acting as the glue to bind them together has to be the Search Manager.

So who should be on the project teams? There has to be a strong business focus to this team to ensure that the search engine delivers the information needed by the business and is not just another server in the data center. To keep the numbers down consider a three level approach.

The first level attend the project meetings. They need to have the time available not only to attend the meetings but to work on sub-projects between meetings. The second level consists of managers who may have some important contributions to make to the development of the specification, but perhaps only on specific topics. These might include managers with security management responsibilities and the managers of other applications that have embedded search functionality. There should be a mechanism to have excellent two-way communications with these managers, and perhaps they might participate in one or more of the project meetings as appropriate.

The third level has managers who need to be kept informed about the progress of the project, for example other business units, HR (as there could be recruitment or change-of-role decisions) and finance. They need to know about whether the project is on schedule because for example they may need to plan ahead to make space available for the implementation team. Everyone on the three levels needs to know who is on each level. Transparency is a major element of good project governance.

Specification Project Team

This team will be preparing the business case and the specification. There needs to be good representation of the business units that have most to gain from the new search application. In addition there will ideally be an enterprise architecture specialist, the intranet manager (who will not only know about search but will be in a position to support the communications plan for the project), someone with a good knowledge of the network architecture of the company and someone with experience of writing a reasonably complex specification. Add in a project manager, the Search Manager and the project sponsor and the result is a specification project team of perhaps eight to ten people.

Selection Project Team

If the Specification team have done their job well the selection team can have more of an IT focus. Security management is a very important element of a successful implementation and the project team needs to have expertise in identity management and/or systems security. At this stage obviously the procurement department needs to be closely involved. Again the Search Manager and project sponsor will be on the team along with the project manager.

Installation Project Team

The membership of this team is discussed in more detail in Chapter 9, but is included here because this team needs to be set up from the outset of the project.

Project Programme Office

Overall the complexity and importance of this project almost certainly mean that there should be a programme office to manage the transitions between the teams and to hand over to the Search Support Team in due course.

The Global Dimension

The majority of enterprise search implementations will be across more than one country, and probably more than one language. Right from the outset the implications of a trans-country implementation need to be taken into account in setting up the project team that will take responsibility for preparing the specification, undertaking the selection and then managing the implementation. It might be the case that the initial implementation is in the USA and then the application will be rolled out more widely across the company. Even if this wider implementation is not going to be carried out for a year or more all the business and IT units involved need to have some degree of representation on the project team at one of the three levels set out above.

Even a few pages in to this Chapter you would be excused for wondering if all these project teams are really necessary. The answer is YES! Enterprise search is a very high touch application and if successfully implemented and managed will make a significant difference to the working lives of most employees. The risks of buying the wrong solution or not ensuring that there is an appropriate level of resource is very high indeed.

Risk Management

Whatever the project management approach being used a risk management section is very important. Risks are commonly scored by the impact on the project and the probability of the risk event arising. In the case of implementing an enterprise search application there will be not prior experience in the company, and using probabilities from other enterprise application implementations is not a sensible way to proceed. The approach to take is to weight the score heavily in favour of the impact on the project. Just multiplying a three level impact (Low, Medium, High) and a three level probability (Low, Medium, High) gives equal weight to both parameters.

For a search implementation a five level impact score is advisable that relates to the completion date of the project:

1. Will extend the project by no more than one month
2. Will extend the project by two months
3. Will extend the project by three – four months
4. Will require the project to be halted while a new project plan is developed
5. Will require the project to be terminated

The reason for taking this approach is that if the due diligence has been carried out on user requirements then the only risk that cannot be quantified is if the vendor either goes out of business or is acquired and there is an inevitable period of re-assessment and re-negotiation of the contract.

Other risks that need to be taken into account include:

- A change in the project sponsor
- An inability to manage secure access to confidential information
- The loss of the Search Manager

- Lack of internal IT resources because other enterprise implementations have been given a higher priority
- At the Proof of Concept stage none of the vendors meet the core requirements
- Poor quality content and/or metadata means that there is little perceived improvement in search quality
- Substantial business change, such as a merger or acquisition
- Risk scores are usually the product of impact and probability. Because there will be little or no previous search procurement experience it may be better to set out the impact and then the expertise available to address the issue should it arise.

Project Schedule

Selecting and implementing an enterprise search application can take some time to bring to completion. The typical steps and the time that should be allocated to each step are set out in Table 8-1.

Table 8-1. Typical steps

Step	Duration
Determine and document user requirements	2 months
Develop a short list of vendors/developers/implementation partners	
Visit other companies who have recently implemented an enterprise search application	
Prepare the Request for Proposal	1 month
Circulate to the short list of vendors and allow time for the response	1 month
Assess the proposals	1 month
Set up the Proof of Concept	1 month
Invite vendors to participate	
Undertake Proof of Concept evaluation and select a preferred vendor	2 months
Negotiate a contract	1 month
Prepare for installation	1 month
Implementation and acceptance testing	1 month
Initial roll-out and assessment of user experience	2 months
Total time	13 months

Adding in a Request for Information round will extend this project schedule by a month, and there could be additional time needed for the proposal preparation and evaluation stages if there are some regulatory requirements for public and Government procurement schedules.

It could be that in the case of one or more of these stages some reduction in time could be achieved, but it would be wise to work on the basis that from the time the decision is taken to implement a new search application to the time that users begin to use the fully-configured application is likely to be at least a year. During this time the business may have changed its objectives and/or there could have been changes to other enterprise applications, and it is advisable to have a major project review before the proposals are assessed to ensure that the specification is still valid.

Of course it will be different for your organization; it always is! You will look at this schedule and change the word 'month' into 'week' for many of the project stages. There are three possible outcomes:

- You will reduce the elapsed project time but the search application will not deliver to requirements and expectations.
- Costs and resources will be based on a shorter project time, but if the schedule cannot be met then there will be cost over-runs and members of the project team may have to go off to other projects.

The choice is yours.

Writing the Specification

The first decision to be made is whether to go straight to a Request for Proposal (RFP), also known as an Invitation to Tender (ITT) or to prepare a Request for Information (RFI) as a means of reducing the number of proposals received. The decision depends on the level of expertise that the company has, and also whether there is an intention to go down an open-source route. In the case of open-source applications there are an increasing number of development companies, and a preliminary shortlisting can be valuable. The route taken will also depend on the procurement policy of the organization, especially in the European Union where there are some EU-wide public sector procurement rules.

Most companies will have a preferred way of writing a specification. In this section the information that vendors will expect to see in the specification is set out. The order in which is appears in the specification is unimportant. With every one of these sections it is important to present not only the current state of affairs but what the expectations are going to be over the three years of operation after implementation.

The Story So Far

Some background on the decision to go out to tender for an enterprise search application should be included. Vendors appreciate a high level of honesty at this stage because it enables them to judge what their approach should be in presenting the benefits of their solution.

Content Scope

This section should go into some detail about the volumes of content to be indexed, in terms of both raw storage but also an indication of the number of documents, the rate of addition of new content and how quickly this new content needs to be able to be searched. Also in this section the main file formats need to be listed, and of course any languages that need to be indexed and/or supported with language-specific interfaces. Even if the initial implementation is going to be for text-based content almost certainly the development of content analytics and search-based applications is going to create new opportunities and requirements in the not too-distant future.

User Expectations

The word 'expectations' is used rather than requirements because this section needs to cover the expectations of all the stake-holders. These expectations cover not just the search experience but the time-scale for the implementation and the ability to customize the search application without any further support from the vendor. If these are not set out in the specification they will do so at the selection meetings and can easily derail the entire process.

Information Systems Architecture

Hardware requirements can be a significant cost element, especially storage and network bandwidth so the current information systems architecture does need to be clearly set out. Again future intentions need to be clearly signaled, especially intentions to move towards cloud-based applications.

IT Partnerships

Many companies already have long-term contracts with systems integrators and have out-sourced development to companies based in India and some other countries. For a vendor some of these partnerships could be advantageous and others may present challenges because they may themselves have agreements with other search vendors. Included in these partnerships should be information about enterprise contracts with major suppliers of software and services, notably IBM, Oracle, Microsoft and HP, all of whom have significant interests in search technology.

Internal Development and Support Resources

This is especially important in the case of open-source projects. Vendors want to get a sense of who they will be dealing with at the installation and implementation stages, and it is advisable to present the corporate expertise as short profiles of individual members of staff. Almost certainly there will be other enterprise development projects taking place at the same time as the search implementation so there could be some potential issues about availability over the six-nine month period that it might take to fully deploy the search application.

Security and Identity Management

The corporate approach to identity management and security management, both of access to the search system and also at a document level should be set out in detail. If there some current issues, or changes are going to made to system security (perhaps to accommodate access over mobile devices) then these need to be highlighted in this section.

Federated Search Requirements

The vision for enterprise search is that it will be able to search across multiple repositories and applications and present a ranked list of relevant information. This is certainly possible, but the costs and other implications are considerable. Although there may be some fine print in the functional requirements the expectations for federated search should be highlighted in the initial section of the specification. Also in this section should be a list of all current search applications (for example SharePoint 2010) and what the current plans are for upgrading these applications.

People Databases

One of the most valuable benefits of enterprise search is being able to find individuals by name and by experience and expertise. In this section details of any HR databases should be given, together with the extent to which the company requires the enterprise search application to meet the requirements of national and EU-level data privacy legislation.

Project Timetable

The stages of the overall project programme should be clearly described, including what will be expected at the Proof of Concept stage, as this will be quite labor-intensive for the vendor.

Functional Specification

The first piece of advice is not to write a detailed functional specification that ends up with perhaps 500 individual functional requirements. This was certainly the case in a specification produced by a large financial institution a few years ago. There are a number of reasons why preparing a very detailed functional specification is not going to improve the chance of finding the best fit.

Most search vendors do not have a large team of people waiting around to prepare responses to RFPs which drop into their email boxes. They will look at the time it is going to take them to respond and they may well decide that filling in a response to 200 or more boxes is not a good return on their investment. Either they will not reply or they will just go through the motions and cut and paste content from the last such RFP they received

Probably at least 80% of all requirements can be met, to some extent, by all search vendors. The important functionalities will then be lost in the noise of the common features. There is no point asking for a list of all the file formats that the vendor is able to support when what is needed is absolute confirmation that the file formats that are important to the company can be handled with certainty.

The time it is going to take the project team to review each proposal is going to be considerable. By the time the last of ten proposals have been reviewed the team has almost lost the will to live and is not looking carefully enough at the proposals.

The approach that should be taken is to focus in on some areas where there are some differences of approach between vendors (and this includes open-source suppliers) and which therefore enable the team to come up with a well-considered short list for more detailed review.

Connectors and APIs

If the search application needs to be able to index content from all required repositories or provide federated searches across applications then any concerns about the capability of the vendor to achieve this need to be identified at the outset. As with so many elements of search it is not just whether the connectors and APIs are available but the extent to which they have been deployed successfully in other clients.

Federated Search User Interfaces

Even if the connector technology is available just how the results presented on the user interface is equally important. There are a number of different approaches on offer and this is where you should be expecting to see some detailed screen shots of installations and ideally even a video demonstration of real interfaces.

Index Freshness

The challenge for all search vendors is to be able to update the index with new content in a time that matches the requirement by the customer to be able to find recently indexed content. As with federated search there are various approached to index updating.

Filters and Facets

Most vendors now offer filters and facets to help users drill down into a set of results. It is important to check the extent to which these filters and facets can be modified by the Search Support Team without the need to involve the support team from the vendor.

Taxonomy and Metadata Management

Most companies will have some form of taxonomy, even if it is just a list of controlled terms or a list of approved abbreviations. Integrating these into the search application can be a challenge and understanding the way in which this can be achieved is important to clarify right from the outset.

Search and System Logs

If you cannot measure something then you cannot manage it, and that is certainly the case with search logs and system logs. Many vendors will have some standard search logs which are a good place to start, but creating just the views needed to manage your implementation could be a step too far and result in the need for the vendor to develop some customized reports

Entity Extraction

This topic has been covered in some detail in Chapter 6. Some vendors buy in third-party products from companies such as Teragram and Basis Technologies and others have developed their own entity extraction algorithms. As is so often the case with enterprise search it is not what is supplied with the initial install that matters as the ease with which changes can be made to the rules and algorithms on the basis of the experience gained following the initial implementation.

Questions for the Vendors

So far we have covered the base-line information that vendors will value and some of the functional requirements that need to be clarified. In addition there are some questions that need to be asked of vendors, the replies to which can be very valuable input into the evaluation process.

Risk Assessment

Any enterprise search implementation involves risk. The organization itself has never implemented search on this scale before and so has little idea of the specific risks there may be with the implementation of the search application from a specific vendor. However the vendor will have carried out a substantial number of implementations and should have a good idea of the risks and issues involved. It can be very illuminating to ask what the vendor sees as the main risks to a successful implementation based on the specification provided, and how it will work with the project team to ameliorate these risks?

Project Schedule

It is not easy for the vendor to provide a definitive answer to the question about the duration of the implementation project, but it should certainly know how long it took in the case of other clients. Ask the vendor to provide a case study of a similar implementation, setting out the timetable from the time of starting the proof of concept and including information on the resources that both the vendor and the client contributed to the implementation.

Project Management Methodology

The company may have its own approach to managing projects, often based on PRINCE2. A clear statement of the methodology used by the vendor will enable potential project management and communications issues to be identified at the earliest possible opportunity. Of particular importance is how red flag issues will be identified and dealt with. It is reasonable to ask the vendor to include some typical project management forms and procedures in the response to the proposal. Search implementation is quite complicated, as you will see from the next chapter, so the project management approach is a critical success factor.

Upgrade Release Schedule

It is useful to gain some understanding of the application development road-map of the search vendor. The search business is highly competitive and there is an understandable reluctance to go too public with a product road-map. Nevertheless there should be some element of comfort in seeing what the product roadmap might be and so assess the impact the future development possibilities.

Supporting a Global Implementation

The challenge with enterprise search is providing installation and implementation across multiple countries. The level of representation of search vendors globally is very variable. US vendors may have a representative in Europe but their task is pre-sales and some customer support. The technical teams are back at headquarters and that could be many time zones away. Global support issues need to be identified at an early opportunity. There is no point in acquiring a complex search application if the technical support cannot be effectively managed by the vendor or the vendor help-desk is based in the USA and so there is only a small time slot open for EU-based search operations.

User Groups

Perhaps surprisingly currently there are not many vendor user groups. One of the un-derstandable reasons for this is that the installed base in any single country is too small to support a national user group. With the technology now available there should at least be a regular virtual user group. The point here is to be certain about the quality of the dialogue between the vendor and the customer. You want to know about upgrades and bug fixes as soon as possible and also to feel that you have an influence on the way in which the search application is developed.

Key Employee Strategy

Even in quite large search vendors there are some employees engaged on either devel-opment or on installation that have accumulated a significant amount of expertise. Asking about whether the search vendor has a key employee strategy in place so that if one of these employees leaves the company is exposed in either development or in im-plementation expertise. Of the two skill sets implementation expertise is more impor-tant because it could directly affect the schedule and the quality of the implementation.

License and Support Costs

In the initial proposal it is unlikely that there will be more than an indication of the full cost of the implementation. Expect for Google and some other appliance vendors the algorithm for calculating the final amount payable will be difficult to unravel. Fixed cost contracts are very rare as there are so many unknowns from the viewpoint of the vendor at the stage of preparing the proposal. The only way to gain at least some sense of the final cost is to set out some scenarios for expansion routes and get at least some estimates from the vendors, but these will all be couched in very vague terms. It is not that they are being difficult, just cautious about committing themselves to a set of unknowns.

Reference Sites

This is always a sensitive subject. The number of variables is such that assessing the extent to which an implementation and search satisfaction at one customer is going to provide any degree of insight into the performance in your case is asking far too much. What is worth exploring is the way in which the vendor and the reference customer worked together. Were there good channels of communication and were promises made that were not kept?

Training

Some training can be delivered on the vendor premises on a test server but there will be a need for hands-on training during the installation and implementation stages. There should be a clear statement of how this is going to be carried out, and the prior experience that is expected of the staff being trained. Training employees up to be trainers themselves seems to be a smart idea but it is very important to make sure that the staff have the skills and time and incentives to be trainers of others,

Building the Vendor Short List

As the list of vendors in Appendix B of this book illustrates there are around 80 search software vendors, but in reality the list of potential suppliers is a lot smaller. This is because many of the vendors are not in a position to support a multi-country implementation, or even a large-scale implementation in a single country which is many miles and time zones away. Many of these companies will have partnerships with sales and possibly implementation companies in other countries but often only limited business is conducted through these channels.

At the other end of the scale IBM, Oracle, HP and SAP have global sales, implementation and support networks, so in theory they should be in an ideal position to provide a multinational offering. The reality can be different. In 2012 and well into 2013 these companies are and will be digesting the acquisitions they made in 2011 and 2012, and it may not be clear exactly what is on offer at what price. If your company already has enterprise agreements with these companies then it would be foolish not to consider what they have to offer.

A good starting point is the Enterprise Search Report published by the Real Story Group, based in Washington DC. This report, one of many published by RSG, provides detailed profiles of the leading enterprise search vendors.

The 2012 report has profiles of:

- Adobe
- Apache
- Coveo
- Exalead
- Google
- HP-Autonomy
- IBM
- Lexmark - Isys-Search
- Microsoft
- Oracle
- Recommind

- SAP

This is not a complete list of 'enterprise search vendors' but the merit of the report is that the detailed profiles highlight some of the issues that need to be taken into consideration when selecting a search application.

The search industry is also covered by a number of other consulting companies, notably The 451 Group, Forrester, Gartner and International Data Corporation. Many consulting companies try to summarize the leaders and laggards in a graphical format, but using these as the basis for a shortlist is not a good idea because search applications are far too complex to reduce to a two-dimensional diagram.

Another useful approach is to post a request for advice to the Linkedin Enterprise Search Professionals Group. There are currently over 7000 members. Many of the replies may come via the private response route!

Many companies score the proposals they receive to help develop a short list to move onto the next stage. In the case of enterprise search the complexity of the functionality means that the differences between vendors in terms of delivering functionality are going to be small. You may end up with scores of 235, 246, 297 and 299. Dropping off the two low scores does not make sense, as each member of the team will be scoring the proposals with little previous experience of enterprise search.

This is why a multi-stage approach is the best option, with an initial Request for Information to come up with a list of perhaps six vendors to whom the Request for Proposal is then sent out. The aim should be to end up with no more than three vendors for the Proof of Concept stage.

Using a Consultant

There are consultants who maintain a strictly vendor-neutral approach to vendor selection projects, offering services from the user requirements work right up to supporting the project team in advising on the selection of a search application. These consultants also provide ongoing support post-implementation but very rarely get involved in the implementation work. One of them is writing this book!

Using a Implementation Partner

As described in Chapter 7 many of the larger systems integration companies offer search implementation services. In addition there is an increasing number of specialized search implementation companies, some of whom will provide development services for open-source search applications. Most of these companies will be in a position to do everything from the user research through to implementation. It may seem a very convenient way to manage a search project but there is a substantial risk of ending up with an installed application and no knowledge of how it works and how it should be managed. Using an implementation partner should indeed be a partnership and organizations should be well aware of the benefits and risks of any IT implementation partnership.

If using a partner is attractive in terms of speed of implementation and overcoming a lack of internal expertise the first two questions to answer are how important speed of implementation really is and will the lack of internal expertise have a negative impact on the long-term management of the search application. It can be instructive to review other implementation partnerships that the organization has established and take the lessons learned into selecting and working with a search implementation partner. If there is no prior experience then the project risk increases substantially.

The big decision is whether the search application is chosen first and then an implementation partner is appointed or the partner is asked to advise on the selection of the search application. Most integration companies work with a small number of search applications with which they have partnership contracts and good access to expertise within the search vendor. This is especially the case with the larger general systems integration companies where search implementation has not been a major business for them in the past. One result of this is that they may not have much experience with the current version of the search software.

Many organizations have an incumbent systems integration partnership, perhaps as a result of outsourcing some elements of IT service provision. Care needs to be taken that the partner concerned has an appropriate level of knowledge of search technology and implementation. In addition if a second partner is appointed just to support the search implementation there is then a triangle of relationships between the organization, the incumbent systems integrator and the search integrator which could be a challenging test the skills of the project manager. This situation is especially likely to arise when the search vendor does not provide implementation services but works through a local partner.

There is no 'best solution' to partner selection. The decision will have both benefits and risks that are dependent on the organizational context, and these need to be worked through in detail before any decision is made.

In the final analysis you need to be certain that the implementation partner has your interests at heart and will be prepared to face up to a vendor problem from your perspective. If the integration partner has a commercial relationship with the vendor then there could be some conflicts of interest. These need to be surfaced, assessed and managed from the outset of the project, not when they arise during the project.

Open Source Software Procurement

So far this chapter has been concerned with commercial software applications though many of the principles are common to open source software selection. However there are some important differences and these are the subject of this section.

The relationship with a commercial search vendor is very much about buying a software product with some consultancy services provided to assist with customization and support. The chances that there will ever be a meeting with the team who have written the application are very small indeed. With open-source software the business model is all about buying consulting services and it is very likely that you will be meeting developers who will go back to the office after the meeting and start writing code. It is possible to carry out the entire development operation in-house, especially if the organization has a strong Java development team, but the missing element will almost certainly be enough understanding how search works to build an application which meets not only current requirements but also future requirements. In-house development can also be hindered by the IT department missing out the user requirements and Statement of Requirements steps and just asking the development team to get on with it. Which they will until a 'more important' project comes along and the priorities of the development team are changed over-night.

Finding potential developers is not difficult. There is a list on the Apache Software Foundation site of people who have contributed code to Lucene and Solr, but many of these may work for large IT companies and will not be available for commercial development work. Using Google and Bing will also result in a list of potential developers, but there are probably fewer developers around than might be expected given the high visibility of Lucene and Solr.

Before beginning to approach potential developers it is important that all relevant managers have signed off on the use of open-source search software. Probably the only other example of open-source software in the organization is going to be a content management application, and these are far less complex than open-source search. With a few exceptions open-source search developers either work for small companies or as members of a virtual team. The statutory accounts of these companies may cause some problems for procurement departments more used to working with large multi-national IT companies.

Another aspect of working with small companies and virtual teams is that they may not be able to start work at once on a project. Indeed if they can it is worth finding out why as competent open-source search developers are in short supply.

There is no point in sending off a highly detailed Statement of Requirements at this early stage. The engagement has to be about both sides building a confidence in each other, and the road to defining the requirements is much more of a collaborative process than might be the case with a commercial vendor. The initial discussions should focus on understanding who the members of the development team would be and what their role would be in the project. The development team will certainly be focusing on what the milestones would be for the project, as it will certainly not be a turn-key development approach with the team going off for a few months and returning with the finished software. The milestones are needed to keep the project on track and also to define payment points. Some developers may work on a fixed-fee basis for a small project but for anything approaching an enterprise development the contract will be on a time and expenses basis. At the beginning of the engagement it might be quite difficult for the development team to give more than a broad estimate of the total cost of development.

The development team will largely work off-site and will need good access to the content that needs to be indexed. This can be a procedural challenge for an organization worried about the leakage of confidential data. It has to be recognized that any transgression on the part of the development team would be immensely painful to the company, to them personally and indeed to the open-source community. The fewer non-disclosure agreements and complex firewall protocols the better. Open-source development works best when all concerned see it as a win-win partnership. This win-win extends to the developers being able to share innovative code with the community.

As well as small independent development teams there are many larger companies, notably LucidWorks, who also offer open-source software development services. The business model may be different but the fundamental elements of a shared commitment to development success remain.

The Best of Both Worlds?

An organization may feel that it wants to hedge its bets and go out to tender to both commercial and open-source solutions. The problem with this approach is that at the evaluation stage the choice will be between apples and oranges. Using a productized open-source solution will make the process a little easier but at all costs resist the temptation to choose between a commercial solution and a bespoke open-source development.

Proof of Concept

This is sometimes referred to as a 'bake-off' and is a very important part of the overall selection process. The objective is to give the potential vendors the opportunity to demonstrate how well their technology works on real corporate information repositories and applications. Preparing for Proof of Concept tests is quite time consuming, and at the stage of writing the proposal the objectives of the PoC tests needs to be set out.

Two test collections should be developed. One of these should be a collection of perhaps 5000 documents against which a number of representative use cases can be run. This collection will enable some key performance parameters to be verified, such as speed of indexing, speed of updating the index, server performance, and the default search user interface. This is sometimes referred to as the Gold or Golden Collection. A proportion of this collection, say 20%, needs to be kept on one side for use in evaluating how the index is updated.

The second should be a collection of documents in every file format that has been identified in the content audit, the objective being to evaluate the performance of the document filters in indexing and in presenting documents in these formats.

Of major importance in a Proof of Concept is how security will be managed. Real ACL lists need to be presented and tested and setting these up can be time-consuming.

An even bigger challenge is to set up a federated search PoC, because this will require the vendor to have the appropriate connectors available. It is probably not worth the effort and a more pragmatic approach would be to assess federated search capabilities at some reference sites. Take careful note of relevance ranking issues.

Carrying out a Proof of Concept tests is probably the most time-consuming difficult and essential element of the selection process. A balance needs to be set between a reasonable level of investment on the part of the vendor on the tests and what the reasonable expectations of the company are for the outcomes of the tests. Typically a PoC may take a week to set up, test, run and evaluate. The conditions for all the vendors need to be the same and the project team from the company needs to be consistent. Servers need to be provisioned and a set of ACLs developed to assess security handling. The vendor team needs somewhere to work that can be kept secure; a desk in an open-desk area is not suitable. The tests may require the participation of IT staff and users in other countries and their availability has to be factored in to the schedule. This is why in Table X the duration of the PoC tests is shown as two months.

Contract Negotiation

It will not be until the contract documents arrive will the full cost of the project become apparent. The vendor will have learned a lot during the PoC tests and will have factored in the impact of discoveries made during the process, especially about the skills of the team that will be responsible for supporting the implementation. It is advisable not to focus just on the cost of the initial installation and implementation. Enterprise search applications are scalable but the costs of scalability can be quite substantial, for example in terms of the costs of developing connectors for specific applications and repositories.

A key factor in the cost structure will be the extent to which the vendor regards the prospective customer as a reference site. If the customer is the first in the sector to invest in a search application then the potential business that could accrue from being able to make a lot of publicity from the win is worth quite a reasonable discount.

An element of the license cost that often only becomes visible at contract stage is the number of servers that are required to establish test, development and production environments and to be able to scale as more content and applications are indexed. Another factor that is often overlooked is the costs involved through an acquisition or through a divestment. Although it is not possible to foretell the future if the organization has growth through acquisition or divestment some scenarios should be discussed at the contract stage that take examples of both into account. This is not just the case of arriving at a 'cost per user' number but about understanding changes in support contracts. Search vendors will always be interested in increasing income but far less so if the acquisition or divestment means a reduction in support income.

It is not uncommon for the contract negotiations to take some time to conclude. Very rarely will a vendor table a fixed price contract. In the table at the beginning of this chapter a period of one month for these negotiations is suggested. That could be optimistic, and it would be wise to build in a float at this point.

Summary

Although organizations will usually have previous experience of selecting and purchasing enterprise-level solutions little of this experience will prepare them for an enterprise search project. The project could easily extend over a period of more than a year from the time of the initial decision to upgrade search capabilities to the day of launch. Bringing in specialist expertise from consultants and from systems integrators will reduce many of the risks but probably not the overall timetable. It is very important to specific what the search application needs to achieve in terms of business impact and not to provide vendors with a long list of features derived from a cut and paste of product documents downloaded from vendor web sites. Undertaking a Proof of Concept is essential. Working out the implications of the lessons learned from the PoC and the complexities of negotiating a contract can take a substantial amount of time and effort.

Further Reading

You'll find some additional information regarding the subject matter of this chapter in the "Further Reading" (page 156) section in Appendix A.

CHAPTER 9

Installation and Implementation

The way in which the installation and implementation of the search application is conducted will be very specific to a particular company. The milestones for an open-source project will also be somewhat different to those for a commercial application. In this chapter a distinction is made between installation and implementation. Installation covers the provisioning and testing of servers and networks, loading all the modules of the search application, checking that user authentication is being managed correctly and undertaking User Acceptance Tests (UAT) that confirm that the base performance criteria are being achieved on a test collection.

Implementation is the process of extending the application to work on live servers and content, and moving the acceptance testing to the search support team and a small group of testers. Overall this could take at least a month to achieve and may be longer with more complex federated search implementations.

Project Management

Installing and implementing an enterprise search application is a complex project with perhaps forty or fifty individual work packages. There will be little or no previous experience of installing enterprise search so this project calls for the best project manager the organization employs or hires. The availability of this project manager will decide when the project can begin, and of course the project will begin perhaps one or two months before the software arrives as the vendor begins the task of fully understanding the content, information architecture and security management environment.

Search implementation projects are characterized by a fairly large number of short-duration work packages that have a lot of interdependencies. Every dependency is a risk and excellent risk management is essential if the project is going to deliver to schedule and objectives. There are many different approaches to project management, and a popular methodology is Prince2. However organizations fail to recognize that a project can be fully compliant with the Prince2 methodology and still fail to deliver the expected outcomes. It is not just about writing a very detailed Project Initiation Document (PID) but having the experience to include all the relevant details. Otherwise comparison with the PID will not flag up issues that need urgent attention.

Vendors will have their own approach to project management and at the earliest opportunity there should be a discussion about how the vendor and customer project plans are going to be integrated into a common plan.

Customer Responsibilities

At the commencement of the project the vendor will identify information and support that they require from the customer. This could include a working area with secure storage, remote access to the customer network and the servers that will be used for the application, and content for indexing. The list will be quite long and a failure on the part of the customer to deliver to agreed schedules could have some significant knock-on impacts on the project because of the dependencies between the work packages. Many vendors and system integrators are small companies and are working on multiple projects so a delay of a week in providing a test sample of content could extend the project by several weeks.

Implementation Schedule

The big question is whether to go for a hard launch (switch off the old and switch on the new) or a soft launch in which both applications are available. The factor that shapes the roll-out plan is how much training and support resource is available. If there is a significant upgrade in capability compared to the current application then users will need support to get the best of the initial version. The initial group of users will also be a test group, so it is not just a question of supporting their use of the application but collecting feedback on how to improve the search experience.

The launch plan also needs to take into account the business cycle. Expecting users to spend time learning the new search application just as the annual business planning cycle starts is probably not a good idea. There could be other upgrades and system launches taking place which should also be taken in to consideration. In public companies the communications team will have more important priorities to deal with than the launch of a new search application.

Even in quite large vendors the team responsible for installing the application is quite small, as specialist skills are needed to cope with the intricacies of the enterprise architecture of the customer. The availability of this team has to be matched to a period of stability with both the content repositories and applications that are going to be indexed by the search application. What might seem to be quite an innocuous upgrade could have a major impact on connector performance.

The overall schedule is then fixed by two dates.

The earliest date that the project can start is when:

- Project manager and search support team in place
- All necessary hardware and access permissions have been established
- Work packages have been agreed and respective roles of vendor and customer have been established
- A full content scope and audit has been completed
- Vendor and customer are confident that security management issues have been addressed
- A communications plan is in place for all stakeholders

The launch date is set by:

- When enough content and functionality is available for users to have a good initial search experience
- Usability tests have smoothed out the initial rough edges to the user interface
- There are enough resources to support the launch, including training and a Help Desk and analysis of the initial set of search logs
- The launch will not take place when another business application is being launched or the business cycle means that users will not have either the incentive or time to make use of the new search application
- There is still enough time to sort out any major problems before a full release to all employees is undertaken

The chances are that there will then not be enough time to undertake all the work needed to deliver the required search experience, so an iterative approach to project scheduling will be required. The point is that beginning the project without being fully prepared and launching the application without adequate content, functionality and support is not to be recommended. Nothing travels faster than news that the launch of a new application, especially one that will be used by the majority of employees, has all the hallmarks of a disaster.

Knowledge Transfer

There is a lot to learn both about the process of search and the technology of the new search application. The worst possible approach is for the vendor team to work in isolation from the search support team. The team not only needs to understand what the search application can offer but also a good knowledge of how the search application works. Even more important is a clear understanding of what the search support team can change without needing to pay for additional consulting days from the vendor.

Forget all about search needing to be intuitive. That may be partially true for end-users but certainly not for the IT team working on the installation and implementation, and for the search support team. Search is complicated and there may well be a requirement to teach about how search works before moving on to the specific elements of the search application that is being implemented.

There should be an initial one or two day training course for the search support team and the project team on the architecture and functionality of the search application so that issues that arise in the course of the implementation can be put into context. Just providing a pile of documentation is not useful.

In addition to this introduction to the project a meeting with a reference client whose implementation has been carried out by the same project team is very valuable. If the vendor is reluctant to come up with a reference client then a proposal to use the LinkedIn Enterprise Search Professionals site to see if any customers have views on the implementation process they would like to share should result in a change of heart. This is so important that it should be written in to the contract. It is all about ensuring that there is a high level of commitment and competence among the vendor project team members.

The Show Stoppers

Two elements of the implementation project have the potential to be major show stoppers and if they are not managed well could jeopardize the success of the project. The first is that the content is as it was described in the content audit and the second is that the security model is as it was described in the initial statement of requirements. The vendor will have carried out some due diligence prior to confirming the contract price but will almost certainly not had the time or support from the organization to do a deep dive into either of these two areas. They represent risks of the highest level of impact on the project and solving problems that were not highlighted in the initial presentations will not only be costly but could mean that the search application cannot deliver to the expectation of users and stakeholders.

The potential problems arising from a failure to have undertaken a full content audit and a full disclosure of security management issues will be especially significant when the plan is to extend the search across multiple applications.

Get Indexing!

Because of the potential impact of content and security issues it is essential to start indexing content at the earliest possible opportunity, even if it is with only a base configuration of the software and on open-access collections. This approach will have the benefit of showing all the stakeholders that the investment in the search application will pay off.

User Interface Design

There is little in this book about user interface design. This is not because it is unimportant but because there are many excellent books on the subject, notably those by Marti Hearst, Peter Morville, Tony Russell-Rose and Tyler Tate, and Greg Nudelman.

The challenge is summed up very concisely by Tony Russell-Rose:

> The results page plays a crucial role in the search experience, conveying to users a response to their information needs, and engaging them in a dialogue that guides them along their information journey. By drawing on a broad repertoire of layouts, views and configurations, it can support a variety of search modes and contexts. And even when there are no results to return, it can still facilitate productive exploration and discovery.

Usability and Accessibility Testing

When a project schedule slips the work packages that almost always get cut are the usability tests on the user interface design. Usability tests are as important as any other element of the search implementation process, and setting high standards for the tests at the implementation stage provides benchmarks for tests undertaken later in the life of the search application when new applications or new facets are added to the search scope. Accessibility is also important to test. This is the extent to which users with a range of visual and physical disabilities are able to use the search application. Often the terms 'usability' and 'accessibility' are used interchangeably but they refer to different aspects of the user experience.

Disaster Recovery Tests

Effective disaster recovery is essential in a search application because there is a significant danger of content being crawled but not indexed. It is important to actually test the disaster recovery procedures under real-life conditions. Often search disaster recovery comes down the bottom of the list of priority applications to restore. However a search application will still be able to identify information from its index even if the core application is not running.

Help Desk

The implementation process will touch a lot of other applications and the team on the IT Help Desk need to be involved at the earliest possible opportunity. The technical team from the vendor needs to talk in technical jargon not only to the Help Desk team but to other IT specialists. Using the project manager to relay messages is going to confuse rather than communicate. Servers in particular tend to have shorthand descriptions linked to a Configuration Management Database. One of the few pleasures that IT managers have is devising up with naming conventions that are unambiguous to internal staff but have no meaning at all to external staff to reduce any chance of inadvertent or deliberate hacking. Every server that might somehow be affected by the search implementation needs to be identified. This is especially important when indexes and repositories are maintained on a remote and/or virtual basis. The name that Corporate IT uses for a server in India could be very different from its local description. This should not be the case but all too often it is.

Metadata Management

Good search needs good metadata. It is as simple as that. Part of the implementation plan should be about not only how metadata is going to be added in the future but how legacy content is going to be enriched by metadata. The need for this work will quickly become obvious as the initial implementation crawls, indexing and queries are undertaken.

At a minimum content needs to have:

- A good title
- A good file name
- A date that defines when the content was released for use
- Correctly spelt names of the authors

In addition a good summary will be a source of keywords in a defined field, and probably less of an effort to add than working through a lot of drop-down lists in a CMS. This may seem a somewhat heretical view from an information scientist but what might be ideal and what can be accomplished in a very busy and probably under-staffed department are two different things.

Communications Plan

From the moment the contract is agreed a communications plan needs to be implemented, which means that it should have been developed well before the contract is signed. There is a role here for Internal Communications to use every possible com-

---

munications channel available to spread the news about the objectives and progress of the project. The communications plan needs to include ways in which employees can have concerns answered and be able to make contributions to the progress and outcomes of the project.

This level of communications activity may well not have been used for the new finance system or the new customer relationship management system but these applications touched only a relatively few employees. In the case of search everyone with access to a desktop pc, a smartphone and/or a tablet will be looking to assess the outcomes of the investment at the earliest opportunity.

Summary

If the installation and initial implementation are not undertaken with a high level of care and resource allocation the value of the investment in the application will be jeopardized. Implementation planning should be started at the commencement of the project and not at the point of discussing the contract. The creation of test collections is an important element of benchmarking technical and end-user performance.

Further Reading

You'll find some additional information regarding the subject matter of this chapter in the "Further Reading" (page 156) section in Appendix A.

CHAPTER 10

Managing Search

No matter how good the search technology and how closely it meets user requirements without an appropriate level of investment in the search support team the chances of continuing to meet the requirements of the organization and the individual requirements of users are going to be close to zero. My main objective in writing this book was to get this message across as clearly as possible.

Implementing search should never be 'a project'. The work of ensuring that users continue to have high levels of search satisfaction will never come to a close. Each week, and perhaps even most days, there will be something that needs attention. The role of the search support team is not just to be reactive but to anticipate when changes to the search application need to be made, or to identify a training requirement that will address an issue that is just starting to show up on the search logs and user satisfaction surveys.

The strange thing is that for other applications organizations seem more than ready to provide a high level of support staff. Research from Computer Economics Inc. in 2011 suggested that the median level of support for an Enterprise Resource Planning application is 75 users per member of the support team. Translate this into 20,000 users of a search application and the result would be a requirement for a support team of nearly 600 people! Research carried out by Findwise suggests that a median figure for an enterprise search team is probably 300 people!

Search Support Team Roles

It is not possible to state definitively how many people there should be in a search support team. Some of the factors that need to be taken into account are:

- The level of support provided by the vendor, systems integrator or external development team

- The extent to which search is a business-critical application and a delay of even a few hours in fixing a problem could have an impact on corporate reputation
- The number of different business activities, each of which is likely to have its own technical language and use cases
- The extent to which the search application has to cope with more than a single language
- The global distribution of search users
- The global distribution of indexed repositories
- The level of local technical support
- The extent to which IT Help Desks are able to provide support for search users
- The volume of searches, which will have an impact on the scale of the search logs
- The extent of federated searching, which tends to throw up more challenges for search support teams than almost any other aspect of search implementation

Not all members of the search team will be engaged full time on supporting users, but overall there are some well-defined roles and responsibilities that need to be covered.

The key roles that need to be filled in a search support team are the following:

Search Manager

This role is not an IT role but instead requires a very good understanding of how information is used in the business, with a particular emphasis on unstructured information. The Search Manager might usefully have a background in information science or business intelligence applications but the key success factor is that they understand the language of the business. Excellent project management skills are also essential as this is going to be a complex installation and any failure to deliver will be very visible to the majority of the workforce.

As well as managing the search team the Search Manager needs to maintain a close working relationship with the search vendor and the search integrator, not only so that problems that arise with the search software are quickly addressed but also to gather and assess the experience of these partners from other installations. Sadly it seems that many vendors are unwilling to bring their customers together to share experiences and good practice.

Search Technology Manager

This is an IT role and the person concerned will be responsible for assessing server and network performance, crawling schedules, load balancing, back-up and disaster recovery. In a multi-national company this may require treading on the operations of national

IT managers. Typically an ERP or CRM application is country or at most regional specific, but enterprise search will be global from the outset and requires 24/7 availability. This may require an investment in hardware from the centre which cannot be justified by a national IT operation.

As a result this can be a 'management' role as much as a technical role as the person concerned has to have the experience and the authority to ensure that things happen in operations over which they have no direct control. Just agreeing this can be a lengthy process of political negotiation, and needs to start right up front, and not when the software is about to be installed.

Another important responsibility of the Search Technology Manager is to manage information security, user authentication and user permissions. It is usually not until an enterprise search application is implemented that all sorts of 'confidential' information is found lurking on shared drives.

Finally this role should take responsibility for API management and documentation Effective enterprise search across multiple applications will require some complex APIs which have to be kept under review as the individual applications are upgraded or restructured. The scope of this role also includes tracking the performance of document filters and connectors, both of which can be susceptible to even small changes in application configuration.

Search Analytics Manager

One of the critical success factors for enterprise search is the quality and regularity of the interpretation of search analytics. The volume of the search reports is very extensive. In one global consulting business around 500,000 searches were being carried out each month. One of the most important tasks for the Search Analytics Manager is to work through the searches which resulted in zero hits being found. If the assumption is made that only 0.1% of searches failed to find anything then this still represents a total of 500 searches a month, or around two each working day. Finding out why this search has failed may require some detective work, and certainly some feedback to the search user.

Search Information Specialist

Good search needs good consistent metadata, and yet metadata management is not given the priority it needs in an enterprise search implementation. As has been highlighted earlier relevance ranking invariably places more weight on words and concepts in the title of the document.

If the title is missing nor is not well written then the relevance of that document may be decreased even if in fact the value to the user of the content of the document is high. The Information Specialist ideally needs to have a background in information science or in librarianship so that they have a fundamental training in metadata management and in the benefits and challenges of taxonomies.

A good taxonomy can be of considerable value in enhancing the search dialogue, but the development of taxonomies requires specialist skills, especially where a company is working in more than one language. Some search products (and Verity was a good example) offer customers support in the development of taxonomies, but it has to be realised that at present, and perhaps for some years to come, a totally computer-based approach to taxonomy development is not likely to be available. Of course some search vendors decry taxonomies and say that their product does not require such an artefact from the world of library science. That may or may not be the case, so the Information Specialist should have the skills to determine the truth in this statement in terms of the particular collections that the company wishes to make searchable.

Another responsibility of the Search Information Specialist should be to conduct some standard test queries on topics that emerge from the search logs as popular searches. A lot can be learned from these queries, and they are a good basis for developing some best bets for common search queries.

Search User Support Manager

This person acts as the user-facing member of the team, undertaking training and usability testing, and providing feedback from surveys on the performance of the application. Although in theory search applications claim to need only minimal training the reality is that this is not the case, especially where federated searching is being carried out. Users may not fully appreciate the provenance of the various information repositories being searched and will need good guidance notes and suitable Help documentation on the search application.

Another important role for the User Support Manager is to develop and maintain good communications channels with users, perhaps using a section of the intranet, a wiki or a series of blog posts to keep everyone informed about the on-going development of the search application, highlight 'tips and tricks' and report back on the solutions that have been found to the inevitable range of problems that have been identified.

In summary this analysis indicates that there are five search team roles:

- Search Manager
- Search Technology Manager
- Search Information Specialist
- Search Analytics Manager

- Search Support Manager

At the specification and selection stage not all of these are required full time. In principle it might be thought that there is no requirement for the Search Analytics Manager at this stage but given the importance of analytics they need to be involved in ensuring that the analytics requirements are fully specified and are tested in the Proof of Concept stage.

Even at the early stages of implementation the team may be able to cope on a 'part time' basis but the evidence is that this approach is not sustainable for very long. It is important to remember that search touches everyone in the organization who has access to a desktop, and any failure to locate business-critical information on a timely basis could have serious implications for the organization.

Enterprise search vendors tend not to be too explicit about the scale of support needed following installation of their software. There is a concern that prospective customers are aware of how much support is needed they may not proceed with the purchase. Even if the purchase of the software has been made some time in the past there should be no reason why a search vendor should not be willing to share information about the size and roles of search teams in other customers.

Supporting Global Enterprise Search

The support requirements are significantly greater when enterprise search is rolled out globally. There is likely to be a need for an Information Specialist for each major content language, especially in the case of German (where word length and complexity can raise some novel issues) and of course in ideographic languages such as Chinese, Japanese and Korean. These and other languages (Finnish is the classic example) will need attention paid to stemming and lemmatization and to seemingly simple issues such as the way that organisational names (such as OECD) appear differently in French (OCDE). This may not be a full time position but certainly the expertise needs to be available to the search team.

For similar reasons there is a good case to be made for an Analytics Manager for each business area in a highly diversified global corporation. The search terms used for one section or subsidiary of the business may well be very different from those in others. Investment banking and retail banking would be a good example.

Certainly there has to be a Search Support Manager in each major country, or at least each region (Europe, Asia/Pacific, North America) and language issues have to be born in mind. Although people may well speak several languages in business situations they will prefer to search in the language in which they have the best command, so Spanish language search and support in South America is very important.

As a result the numbers can add up:

- One Information Specialist (IS) for each major language (x)
- One Search Analytics Manager (SAM) for each business area (y)
- One Search Support Manager (SSM) for each major country (z)

Core search team of at least three for search management and vendor relationship management:

Team size = x(SAM)+y(SSM)+zC+3

So for an organisation operating in English, French and German, with two main business areas, and with significant business operations in the USA, France, Germany, Dubai, New Dehli, Seoul and Beijing the numbers work out at:

Team size = 3(IS) + 2(SAM) + 7 (SSM) + 3

That totals 15 members of staff, and for the purposes of this calculation local IT support has been excluded.

This may seem quite a considerable team, but it can be interesting to find out how big the support teams are for enterprise applications such as an HR portal, an enterprise resource planning application a business intelligence application or a high-end document management application. Why should enterprise search be different?

Creating a Centre of Search Excellence

Many companies set up a global Centre of Search Excellence (CSE) to bring together staff with specialist expertise that may not be available in all business centres. Certainly staff in the Information Specialist and Search Analytics roles may not need to be located in the countries that are supporting, but this is certainly not the case with the Search Support Managers.

The core issue is where this CSE will be located. The obvious answer is in the country where the global headquarters is based and for a great many companies this may be the United States. Then the problem arises of where in the USA given the three-hour difference between the East Coast and the West Coast, and in the case of the latter in particular the resultant time gap between the CSE and operations in mainland Europe of some nine hours – a complete working day.

The decision is not an easy one and needs to take account of:

- The location of staff with the appropriate specialized skills
- The location of the technical support desk of the search vendor and/or implementer

- Which operations/countries are going to present the most complex search enquiries?
- The reporting line for the Search Manager
- The ability to provide real-time access to support from as many of the core geographic areas possible

In the end the decision is likely to be political/organisational than pragmatic, and the downsides of the resulting decision need to be considered in detail and addressed. A Search Center of Excellence can also be helpful in advising subsidiary companies on the selection and implementation of individual search applications.

Search Team Skills

It is not easy to find people with the skill sets needed to meet these roles and responsibilities. In the USA the iSchools have paid more attention to teaching information retrieval and search technology than is the case in Europe, and currently there is no full-time undergraduate course in the world specifically on search and information retrieval. The iSchool at the University of Sheffield is a world leader in information retrieval research, and offers a set of modules on information retrieval to students reading for a degree in Informatics.

Set out below are the topics covered in the course as an indication of the skills that are required in a search support team.

Introduction to Information Retrieval

- The historical development of information retrieval
- Distinctions between search and browse
- Relation between IR systems and databases
- A general architecture of IR systems

Indexing

- The various properties of text documents, such as structure, semantics and metadata
- The concept of indexing, in particular full-text indexing
- The use of a pipeline for pre-processing text documents that includes tokenization, the use of stemming and morphological analysis, selecting subsets of terms based on term weighting and the removal of non-content bearing words

Retrieval and Ranking

- Mechanisms for matching queries with documents, including the use of the inverted index
- Boolean and Best Match (e.g. vector space and probabilistic) modes of retrieval
- The notion of term weighting
- The use of query expansion (through relevance feedback) to maximize the success of matching queries and document representations
- The concept of an inverted index to improve search efficiency

User Interaction and Interface Design

- Understanding the user and their interactions with an IR system
- Supporting user interaction and search user interface design by effective design for interactive search

Evaluation of IR Systems

- The evaluation of information retrieval systems including the different approaches for evaluating systems
- The use of test collections by system developers
- Measures of system effectiveness and user-oriented issues

Web Search

- The basic principles of web searching
- General purpose vs. specialized search engines
- The architecture of general purpose web search engines (e.g. Google)
- Crawling and ranking search results
- Search engine optimization

Enterprise Search

- The evaluation of enterprise search
- Architectures for enterprise search

- Commercially available systems
- Differences between enterprise and web search

Without a good, structured, understanding of these topics within the search team the team will be flying blind, relying on trial and error to improve search performance without understanding either the fundamental principles or the way in which they have been encoded in technology. Is it a risk your organization is willing to take?

Help Desk Management

Because most employees will be using the search application there are likely to be quite a number of calls with queries about the way in which the application seems to be working. A particular challenge of search is the technical complexity of the application, some aspects of which IT departments may not fully appreciate or be able to fix. Relevance tuning is just one example.

Most organizations have some form of IT Help Desk, and larger organizations will have a means of issuing 'tickets' that log the query, track the progress of the resolution and provide a database that can be analyzed for trends in the types of problems that have been encountered with hardware, software and network components.

When it comes to search there are four decisions that need to be made:

- Should the IT Help Desk be the first point of call for any search enquiry?
- Should the IT Help Desk be staffed with the skills needed to handle all search enquires?
- Should there be a separate Search Help Desk?
- If so does the Search Help Desk become the first point of call for search enquiries or act as a support to the IT Help Desk?

The situation becomes more difficult with multi-national operations as there could well be local IT Help Desks with only limited expertise in the main corporate applications. The use of these in some countries may be quite limited but there could be many users of the search application, perhaps in a local language as well as in English.

There is no 'best' model for Help Desk management and much will depend on the skills and resources of the IT Help Desk(s). In the early stages of the implementation of an enterprise search application many of the enquires may be about connectivity and technical performance but as the application beds down there will be more about content and relevance ranking.

Security and Compliance

Search implementations tend to bring up some difficult issues around security management and regulatory compliance. Managing information security is a substantial business and IT task to ensure that documents are only able to be searched and opened by users with the appropriate level of security clearance. It is quite possible that the existing security access protocols will need to be revised to take account of the power of the search application to find information that it is not supposed to find, or more correctly to find it and yet not deliver it unless there is a business/security case for doing so.

It is not uncommon for organisations to highlight the importance of not disclosing confidential information without putting any guidelines in place about how to decide who should be able to have access to specific information. Security has to be managed at the level of individual named employees and their Active Directory metadata.

Potentially even more challenging is meeting the requirements of data privacy legislation, especially if the organisation is subject to EU legislation, which extends to anyone from any country that is working in the EU. The problems of conformance are not just related to intranets. . For example, sending details of an employee's cv to the USA from the UK as the result of a search being carried out in the USA without the consent of the employee could be in breach of the legislation. There is a view by some companies that if they only send information to other sites of their company then the legislation does not apply. This is not the case, and full consent needs to be obtained. This is because there is also a very important distinction between personal information and sensitive personal information in EU legislation.

Sensitive personal information covers:

- The racial or ethnic origin of the data subject
- Their political opinions
- Their religious beliefs or other beliefs of a similar nature
- Whether they are a member of a trade union
- Their physical or mental health or condition
- Their sexual life
- The commission or alleged commission by them of any offence

One of the key issues is that a person has to give their informed consent for this Sensitive Personal Information to be held in a database. Some intranets have an internal staff newsletter. In the interests of good communication there might be a news story about how a member of staff had been ill, but was now coming back to work for a few days a week. This could be regarded as sensitive personal data, as it related to the health of the person, and this information should not be able to be disclosed to anyone outside of the EU.

Many consulting projects, especially in human resources and change management, may require the consultants to check on personal information about employees. Using a corporate intranet from a single site to gain access to this information is likely to be forbidden, and of course if this information is to be held by a third party such as a consulting company, or an outplacement agency, then the employee's permission needs to be sought in advance. The employee also has the right to ensure that the information being held is correct, and this will require companies to implement intranet systems so that the employee can only see their own record, and not that of others. For employees that have left the company this right will extend as long as their file is maintained, which also gives rise to a range of problems, such as the time that a company should reasonably maintain that file.

In reviewing search logs there could be searches on voluntary redundancy, sexual harassment or discrimination or for the addresses of senior staff. All these might be taken as an indication that the person carrying out these searches was planning to take redundancy, sue the organisation for sexual harassment or discrimination, or send the addresses of senior managers to an animal rights activist group. The extent to which search logs might be construed to contain personal information has not yet been tested in the courts.

Data privacy compliance is especially important to take account of in the use of photographs on staff databases. Because a photograph will almost certainly contain information that enables a person's racial or ethnic identity to be inferred (even if incorrectly) staff photographs fall under the provisions of Sensitive Personal Information, and specific permission needs to be sought from each member of staff before their photograph is added. This has to be informed consent, so the member of staff needs to understand the implications and cannot be penalised for not giving consent. The fact that the photograph is on a staff badge does not mean that the photograph can be used for a staff directory. The photograph on a staff badge is there to enable security staff to ensure that the badge is being used by the designated badge holder.

On 25 January 2012 the European Commission published a proposal for a new regulation on the protection of individuals with regard to the processing of personal data and on the free movement of such data. There are some substantial changes proposed to data privacy legislation, in particular the move from a Directive to a Regulation as a means of gaining greater harmony over Member State data privacy implementation. The risks of non-compliance under the Draft Regulation are substantially greater than under the current legal framework and, for the most serious breaches, a national data privacy authority may impose a fine of up to a maximum of 2% of a company's annual worldwide turnover. The new regulatory regime will come into force in 2015/2016 but the work needs to start soon on identifying any potential areas of non-compliance.

It is essential that the advice of lawyers specializing in data privacy is obtained. It is likely that in-house legal teams will not have any substantial expertise in this complex area, especially when an intranet needs to be compliant with a number of different national legislations. Currently around 40 countries have some form of data privacy legislation.

Another area where legal advice is important is the management of a situation when a court requires the company to disclose information for a court case or a regulatory compliance check. Here the processes in the USA are somewhat different to those in most other countries, and are set out in Chapter 26 of the Federal Rules of Civil Procedure. The implications are complex and potentially costly and should not be put on the list of "This can never happen to us."

Search Liaison Specialists

It is important to have excellent lines of communication deep inside the organization. It could be that just one business unit is having a substantial problem with searching across particular repositories, and may not have the time or inclination to report back to the Search Support Team.

This is where the appointment of search liaison specialists in as many business units as possible can be very valuable. They are the eyes and ears of the Team, providing feedback on their own user experience and listening for good news and bad news about the search experience coming from their colleagues. These liaison posts should be visible ones, so that users know who to go and talk to about their search experiences. The liaison specialists should be well trained in the use of the search applications so that they are in a position to provide on-the-spot assistance and to look at failed searches with an experienced eye. This liaison role needs to be included in the job description of the employee. Their manager should appreciate that if the employee moves from their current position then the incoming employee may not be the best fit for the liaison role, and that someone else may need to be found.

Reporting Lines

One of the major challenges in establishing the search team is deciding on the reporting line. It may well be that the team is made up of staff seconded from various departments, and as always in these situations the clarity of the reporting line is even more important than is the case with an intra-departmental team.

The situation with the search team is just the same as with the intranet team. It is difficult to find the optimum position for an intranet team and as a result it may report to Internal Communications, HR, IT or an important Line of Business manager. Having the Search Manager for Enterprise Search report to the Corporate Intranet Manager is not sensible. The scope of enterprise search is potentially much broader than is the case with just intranet search even if in the first instance the search application is implemented for the intranet, and the Intranet Manager may be unwilling to lose the full-time support of their Search Manager as the role develops.

A distinction can usefully be made about the reporting line during the selection and install process (which might well be to the IT Director) and the on-going management of search. In this latter case the requirements are more likely to be driven by the business rather than the IT infrastructure.

The decision is not of course just one of operational responsibility but also of budget. Compared with many enterprise applications enterprise search license costs are concerned are relatively low, and only in very large implementations are the license costs going to be substantially more than $500k. The costs are in the search team, and lines of reporting usually align to budget ownership.

It is not possible to give a definitive recommendation on reporting lines, other than the Search Manager has to be able to make things happen across national and departmental boundaries, and therefore needs the support of a line manager to is able to provide the appropriate level of global support and influence and who appreciates the need for staff support after implementation.

Test Searches

One of the core responsibilities of the Search Support Team is to carry out a range of searches on a regular basis to reproduce the results that others are being presented with. It may be difficult for the Team members to judge relevance but they should be on the lookout for results that look out of place. It may be because they are several years old, have poor titles or are in file formats that may now not be supported by the company.

Another set of searches should be carried out on an agreed set of core documents, such as the main HR policies, pay grades, health and safety topics and corporate publications. Some of these may only be important on a cyclic basis, such as the protocols for carrying out employee evaluations. All of these may be prominently displayed the home pages of other applications (notably the intranet) but that is not an excuse for checking that these documents are easy to find from the search box as well.

It can also be useful to talk to departmental managers about documents that they are responsibile for that should be easily found by employees. Take a list of these documents and see how easy it is to find them using some obvious query terms. The results can be surprising! This process will show where additional metadata needs to be added and previous versions need to be archived.

Best Bets

A feature of many search implementations is the concept of Best Bets. These are documents that are positioned at the top of certain searches to ensure that the results presented are seen in the context of importance of key documents. These best bets need to be linked into specific search terms, so that (for example) any search on the security [risk] always presents the corporate security policy at the top of the search results. The decision on what documents to highlight as Best Bets has to be made in conjunction with the appropriate specialists in the organization. It must never be the sole responsibility of the Search Support Team.

These Best Bets need to be reviewed on a regular basis. Many corporate documents are updated on an annual basis, and the current one needs to be replaced by the up-dated document as soon as it is available. Ideally there should be an owner of every Best Bet, so that if a user has a query about the validity of the Best Bet they can quickly call or email the person responsible for selecting the document. This person may not be the author of the document, because the author may have left the company or moved to another position, or not had the authority to decide that the document is indeed a Best Bet.

Some companies use the concept of Best Bets to highlight experts in the company. A search for [nuclear reactors] in an engineering company may more usefully highlight the name of one or more nuclear engineers than a multitude of standards on how to manage nuclear reactors.

Usability Tests

Usability tests are an important element in developing web sites but there is much less support for usability testing for intranets, search applications and other enterprise applications. Search usability in particular seems often to be totally ignored. The excellent Useit.com web blog of Jakob Nielsen offers very little guidance on search usability. One of the excuses that often given is that since everyone has their own view of what is relevant there is no point in carrying out usability tests. That misses the point about search being a dialog and the need to ensure that the search interface supports the dialog not only up to the point of a set of results being displayed but then supports the user in reducing the total number of results down to manageable list to browse through.

The other common excuse is that usability is too time-consuming and expensive to carry out. The response to this has to be that the company could be at risk from an employee not being able to find the information that could have made a significant impact on business performance. If the company is willing to take that risk then certainly there is no point in carrying out usability tests, but that risk could have a very public impact on the reputation of the company.

Because of the complexity of search user interfaces compared to the options offered on most web and intranet pages usability is not an option but a necessity. The interface situation is going to become even more complex as employees make use of tablet and smartphone devices to access enterprise search applications.

Fortunately some very good books have been written on the subject of search user interface design and testing, and they will be of more assistance than an inadequate summary in this book.

Search Logs

Search logs are a critically important diagnostic tool. Without adequate log analysis any search implementation is flying blind, potentially a waste of investment that has been made in the application. The frequency of analyzing the search logs can only be decided by experience. Monthly may be too frequent for a review of the top searches by query as these will probably not change a great deal from month to month. However a review of searches that seem to have failed should certainly be carried out at least monthly, because a failure to find information could have led to a loss of a business opportunity.

In the case of intranets search logs should be analyzed in conjunction with click statistics on the web pages. In the case of one multinational company the search logs suddenly showed that there were several thousand searches being carried out each month looking for [conference call] or [teleconference number]. It turned out that the internal codes for the corporate teleconference network had been listed on the home page of the intranet, but in a design change these had inadvertently been removed.

The impact on the workforce was considerable, because searching for these terms produced a lot of results along the lines of "Please use the teleconference service for this discussion" but did not provide the number itself. This turned out to be about result #50!

Some of the useful log reports are the following. The number of searches has been arbitrarily set at 50 for the purposes of this book but in practice the number will need to be decided on an ad hoc basis as the scale and value of the log files becomes apparent.

Top 50 Searches by Search Terms/Query

The number is arbitrary but the purpose is to see what are the most popular searches, and some of these could well be a result of poor information architecture on the intranet(s). Even if the enterprise search is working across multiple repositories it is likely that the intranet will be the starting point for the majority of searches. For each term used the reason for it should be fairly obvious. Often the significance of the top terms only becomes visible when the terms are clustered together. In the case of the teleconference number issue there were six different search terms. Individually they came fairly low down the top 50 listing but when aggregated the search theme came third in the overall listing.

Many of the terms in an enterprise search log will be applications, as users search for an application by name or purpose that they have perhaps not used for some time. These need to be discussed with the application owners to understand why users are having to use the search box to find them.

Top 50 Searches Leading to Only a Few or No Results Being Presented

This log will show where there may be gaps in content, or where a search query is being typed incorrectly and the internal directories are not suggesting an appropriate alternate. A user may have chosen the wrong collection or used the wrong acronym for an internal project or product. Enterprise search users will have the expectation that the search application will find something of relevance and finding nothing at all is probably the biggest single reason for not only dissatisfaction with the implementation but possibly a permanent attitude that using the search application is not worth the effort. The end result will be that decisions may be made on inadequate information, to the detriment of business and personal performance.

Top 50 Searches Leading to No Document Being Selected

This is a situation that needs careful scrutiny. Users are being presented with a list of results but either these are so wide of the mark for some reason or the user realizes that they need to go to a section of the intranet or some other application to find the information they are seeking.

Top 50 Most Requested Documents

Some of these may need to be promoted to best bets. A review of the list may also show that users are viewing documents that are in fact out of date or not the best match. These insights can only come from search team members who know the significance of these failures and can allocate the time to find out why users have selected the documents

Top 50 Searches Where More Than Three Pages of Results Were Presented

This analysis should give some indication of where the relevance tuning needs attention, especially if the documents being retrieved were some way down the relevance ranking. There is an expectation that the enterprise search application will be able to deliver relevant information within the first few pages of results. Although unrealistic these expectations need to be acknowledged and solutions found to the user being presented with perhaps 4000 results.

Clicks on Best Bets

Selecting best bets and then ensuring that they remain best bets is an important role of the search support team working closely with experts in the business. Monitoring any fall off on best bet clicks needs immediate analysis because almost nothing is more frustrating to a user than being presented with an irrelevant document at the top of the list of search results

Clicks on Facets and Filters

Monitoring the clicks on the terms in faceted navigation and in filters will show how users are narrowing down a long list of search results for certain queries.

Feedback Forms

There should always be a feedback form on the search page. There is no benefit from having a highly-structured set of questions. Users will not remember the steps they went through and at that moment in time will not want to spend 10 minutes reliving their past. Provide a free-text box and ask users to briefly outline their search experience (good as well as disappointing) and ask for contact information so that a member of the search support team can follow up with them. The form should of course capture the query terms used so that the search can be replicated before, and then during, the discussion with the user.

Training and Support

Training is not an activity that starts and stops in the implementation phase. It is not uncommon for 10% of employees to leave and arrive in the course of a year, and new employees will certainly be stress-testing the search application within minutes of sitting at their desk or switching on their smartphone. The communities that need to be trained and supported include:

- IT department

- Managers of applications that are being indexed

Establishing Good Communications

A good communications strategy is very important in achieving a high degree of user satisfaction. Some of the elements of this strategy might include:

- A search advice section on the corporate intranet, perhaps positioned close to the search box
- A blog from the Search Support Team with success stories, tips for good searching and information about upgrades and enhancements to the search application
- Presentations and workshops given by members of the search support team
- Best bets owners talking about how valuable users have found best bets information
- A wiki which can be used to record issues that have arisen and the progress towards fixing them, and also to post advice on how to get the best from the search application
- Establishing search communities of practice in business units
- Publishing log information on a regular basis

Try to find some search success stories, perhaps by talking to people who were critical of the existing application and are how (we hope) very enthusiastic about the new search application.

Communications is as much about listening as publishing and so users should be encouraged to talk to members of the search support team.

Summary

Managing search is achieved by skilled people who understand the technology and capabilities of the search application working closely with users at all grades, roles and responsibilities and in all locations. That is a tough call and a significant investment but without the skilled people the organization is putting its business activities, objectives and reputation at risk. There is a lot of work to do every single day and with rare exceptions in smaller organizations being a member of the search support team is a full time position.

Further Reading

You'll find some additional information regarding the subject matter of this chapter in the "Further Reading" (page 156) section in Appendix A.

CHAPTER 11

A Future for Search

Writing about the future of search is a challenge because the very rapid pace of technical development could make sections of this chapter look very dated by the time the book is published. My objective in doing so is to illustrate that after a long period of benign neglect it would seem that there is a renaissance in enterprise search. The consensus view is that the rate of growth of enterprise information and data is now so high that action now has to be taken to ensure that the organization can benefit from this information. As the adoption of enterprise search accelerates search vendors will feel more comfortable investing in research and development to bring new functionality to the market.

This chapter summarizes some of the areas in which evidence of this investment will be most evident. In a period of rapid change it is even more important than it has been in the past to have a search strategy that is grounded in business reality and user requirements so that these developments can be assessed in terms of the possible impact they could have on business performance.

1. The Petabyte Challenge

In 2011 McKinsey Global Institute (MGI) published a report on Big Data which indicated that that enterprises around the world used more than 7 exabytes of incremental disk drive data storage capacity in 2010; nearly 80 percent of that total appeared to duplicate data that had been stored elsewhere. MGI also analyzed data generation and storage at the level of sectors and individual firms. It estimate that, by 2009, nearly all sectors in the US economy had at least an average of 200 terabytes of stored data per company (for companies with more than 1,000 employees) and that many sectors had more than 1 petabyte in mean stored data per company.

The combination of low storage costs and a lack of an information management strategy that takes a life-cycle view of information to identify what information can be either archived or deleted, together with a rapid growth in the daily increase of emails, social media, rich media and other information categories as the result of doing business in the 21st Century and the chances of finding any particular item of information are starting to get worryingly low. There are no quick fixes to this situation other than by investing in information management applications such as enterprise search, text and data mining and business intelligence.

2. Industry Consolidation and Expansion

It is too early to gauge the full impact of the acquisitions made by HP, Oracle, IBM, and Lexmark in 2011 and 2012, but it is likely to be a positive one. These major IT companies maintain very close relationships with their enterprise customers and clearly see an opportunity to offer a wider range of search applications to these customers. Shareholders will be expecting to see a return on the investment in these acquisitions, even if in the case of HP it could take some time to achieve. Companies now have a higher degree of security of supply of these search applications, and in addition Microsoft and Google will continue to provide search solutions.

These acquisitions still leave a large number of independent search vendors, most of which are privately held. Investors in these companies can now see an exit strategy. If the technology is good enough then there could be a trade sale possibility, a much easier exit route than going public in the current economic climate.

The entire search industry is going to benefit from the marketing and sales efforts of the major IT vendors and the outcome of research surveys will hopefully convince companies that search is business critical and that the closest possible match between user requirements and technology is essential to maintain business performance.

3. The Impact of Microsoft SharePoint

Microsoft came late to enterprise search and has struggled without success to support the two search applications in SharePoint 2010 and the FAST ESP application it acquired in 2008. Now that the company has taken the decision to withdraw main-stream support from FAST ESP in 2013 it can focus on developing the search functionality of SharePoint. For a significant number of companies SharePoint 2010 has been the first time they have been able to offer employees a good search application, especially so if the company has invested in FAST Search Server for SharePoint 2010 (FS4SP).

The next release of SharePoint is due in 2013 and in mid-July Microsoft released some initial information on FS4SP that is designed to improve both the functionality and administration of the search application. However it is important to remember that FS4SP is optimized for SharePoint 2010 and in the future SharePoint 2013, and that it is not being positioned as a replacement for FAST ESP.

Not only have SharePoint customers now have a better appreciation of the value of search but also Microsoft channel partners have had to become much more familiar with the technology and use of search. This knowledge will gradually result in the emergence of a cadre of search experts that may wish to move out of the integrator role and into a corporate role as search managers and developers.

4. Big Data and Text Analytics

"Big Data" has appeared from no-where to become one of the buzz-words of 2012. The Exalead definition is that a data collection is considered "Big Data" when it is so large an organization cannot effectively or affordably manage or exploit it using conventional data management tools. The size is relative rather than absolute. It is not just a 'Big Company' issue. Another approach at defining Big Data approaches it from the characteristics of Volume, Velocity, Variety and Variability. 'Velocity' takes into consideration both the rate of change of data sets and the impact that even a small data item may have on a much larger data set. 'Variety' is a reflection of the number of different database formats and master data management schemas that may be involved.

In the context of the future of enterprise search there are a number of issues and opportunities arising from the publicity around Big Data. It is putting enterprise search much higher up the list of 'must have' enterprise applications as senior managers start to focus on the ability of the company to find information for probably the first time ever,

The major IT companies see the solution of Big Data problems as a very important market opportunity, hence the acquisitions by Oracle and IBM in particular. Google has launched its Big Query web service and Amazon and Microsoft offer similar services. Autonomy has had a private cloud service for some time.

Companies are starting to discover just how much information they have in databases, and are finding that not only are the existing tools inadequate to meet the potential demand for Big Data analysis but that they have no employees with the skills needed to develop these solutions. In the USA in particular the concept of the 'data scientist' is gaining ground very quickly.

However it is important not to see enterprise search as the 'answer' to managing Big Data. Companies need to be able to find patterns in Big Data and this is where text analytics has a major role to play. With search there is no further transformation to the text when the results are presented to the user. This text must be integrated and transformed before it can be analyzed. Some of the enterprise search vendors do offer text analytics capabilities and will undoubtedly be expanding these in the future but there is also a substantial group of companies that specialize in text analytics, for example Attensity, Business Objects, Clarabridge, ClearForest, IBM, Lexalytics, SAS-Teregram and Synaptica.

5. Business Intelligence and Unified Information Access

Also on the edges of enterprise search are the vendors of business intelligence applications, including Business Objects, Information Builders, IBM, Microstrategy, Microsoft, Oracle and SAP. These applications provide some degree of search capability but their primary role is in proving managers with access to reports and dashboards that enable to track business performance on as near a real-time basis as possible. Again some of the search vendors, for example Exalead, also provide some dashboard interfaces but as with text analytics a significant amount of processing effort is required to integrate, clean and standardize data and information prior to analysis and presentation. Because of the volume of changes that have to be made to the databases on a regular basis (perhaps hourly) business intelligence applications use sophisticated Extract-Load-Transform (ELT) applications supported by Complex Event Processing engines.

In 2008 the Forrester Group published a report on Unified Information Access, making the following observation in the introduction to the report:

> Search and business intelligence (BI) really are two sides of the same coin. Enterprise search enables people to access unstructured content like documents, blog and wiki entries, and emails stored in repositories across their organizations. BI surfaces structured data in reports and dashboards. As both technologies mature, the boundary between them is beginning to blur. Search platforms are beginning to perform BI functions like data visualization and reporting, and BI vendors have begun to incorporate simple to use search experiences into their products. Information and knowledge management professionals should take advantage of this convergence, which will have the same effect from both sides: to give businesspeople better context and information for the decisions they make every day.

Other major consulting companies, notably Sue Feldman at International Data Corporation (IDC) take a similar position. Probably the company doing more than anyone else to get UIA on the agenda of senior management groups is Attivio. The Attivio solution is based on the Apache Lucene open-source software but with a lot of proprietary code on top. Both CEO Ali Riaz and CTO Sid Probstein were at FAST Search and Transfer prior to its acquisition by Microsoft. It is indicative of the potential for UIA solutions that Attivio gained an investment of $37M late in 2012.

As with 'Big Data' the term 'Unified Information Access' has no concise definition but it is indicative of an increasing level of integration between text-based enterprise search, business intelligence, content analytics, text and data mining and big data applications.

Over the next few years the 'edges' between enterprise search, text analytics and business intelligence applications will become increasingly blurred but underneath the user interface they remain quite distinct applications and it is doubtful that any vendor, even IBM or Oracle, will be able, or even wish to be able, to offer a universal application.

6. Mobile Search

We are only at the very beginning of the mobile revolution. In 2010 it looked as though it was all about corporate-supplied smartphones and just two years later it is about the corporate use of personal smartphone and tablets. Mobile access is all about search, and about delivering information not just documents. For some years now search applications have extended across the entire desktop surface with facets and filters. This type of user interface has value for certain use cases, but not for mobile use. Screen space is at a minimum and the use of every pixel has to be optimized.

As a result mobile user interfaces are going to move in novel directions and in doing so will stimulate innovation in the desktop interface. For mobile use context is everything. This is not just about location-specific context but about searches that may have been carried out in the previous hours or days, and not necessarily on the mobile device itself. A sales manager may well have updated a set of customer profiles on a desktop or a tablet but now needs the latest possible information on the customer as they wait in a reception area with no more than a click or saying 'Here' into the smartphone.

This type of requirement is also going to increase the requirement to create and store search profiles and to be able to retrieve results sets from earlier searches, something that has not been given much attention.

Siri, the voice-command feature of the Apple iPhone and iPad, has remarkable capabilities even in its initial release, and mobile requirements will undoubtedly stimulate the development of natural human interfaces, such gestures and eye-movement, which will be transferred to desktop devices sooner rather than later. Some search vendors, notably Isys-Search, have taken a bottom-up approach to designing mobile search applications, whereas others are still trying to adapt full-screen approaches.

The interface with mobile search will be either voice, a single finger or a wave of the hand. These natural interfaces will almost certainly migrate from mobile to the desk top. The office of the future may end up looking very like the vision presented in the US TV series Crime Scene Investigation (CSI) where the forensic police team can call up any number of applications through a touch of a screen and drill down into the data the same way.

7. Cross-Session Search

Because relevance is defined in terms of a single user it is easy to ignore the situation where the same user is carrying out multiple searches on perhaps quite different topics and would value the search application being able to integrate the different searches together. A use case might be where an engineer has been presented with the need to design a particular type of bearing. There are many approaches to this problem and the engineer may want to explore each of these individually and then integrate the best of the solutions together in a desktop environment rather than cutting and pasting from a set of printed search results.

An extension of this use case is where members of a development team have conducted searches using their own particular skill and knowledge sets and now wish to integrate them for the use of their colleagues. As more work is carried out in virtual teams in multiple locations the ability to integrate multiple searches, and then have the master query and result set updated on a periodic or ad hoc basis is going to emerge as an important business requirement.

8. Social Search

As with so many other aspects of search the term 'social search' is not well defined. The role of enterprise search in the effective use of social media is going to be increasingly important. As the number of blog and wiki channels increase and as more work is carried out in collaborative workspaces, the challenge of tracking new items of information that are relevant to any of the multiple tasks that we carry out each day is going to be increasingly difficult to manage using RSS and other alerting feeds. The solution will be to use search as a means of filtering perhaps a hundred different channels to provide a ranked list of newly added relevant information. This use of search is already well developed by companies providing press alerting services. In the enterprise the search application will need to cope with the language of social media, which will inevitably make use of colloquial language and shortened forms of words and expressions, especially in the case of microblogging.

Another view of social search might better be described as social context search, where the search application is taking account of documents and blogs that the user has written, recent searches they have carried out and meetings that are in their calendars. The aim is both to improve the quality of search results and to alert the user to relevant content. Managing the potential overload of information will be a challenge, and will require organizations to invest in training employees to get the best out of these applications.

9. Federated Search

Federated search, the ability to search for information across multiple repositories and applications and then provide an integrated set of results, is a fundamental requirement of enterprise search. The usual model is for a module of the master search application to send the query to the search applications in each of the target repositories. The results from each are then integrated in some way and presented to the user. In theory it is easy, and in practice it is extremely difficult. Each of the individual search applications will have calculated a relevance ranking on the basis of the content in the repository, so normalizing the results to provide a rational overall ranking is not a reliable solution. There are almost certainly going to be performance delays, especially if the repositories are located around the world, and these performance delays will be acerbated if the repositories have different security models. Single sign-on for all applications is still rarely achieved.

Then there is the challenge of de-duplicating content from the various repositories. There are solutions for this when a single language is being used, but the situation is much more complex with multiple languages.

Another option is to create a master index of all repositories, search the master index and then download the relevant items from each repository. This option runs into some serious index performance management challenges.

A substantial amount of research and development is being undertaken into achieving good performance from federated searching as this is a core requirement of unified information access and search-based applications. Despite the best endeavours of search vendors high-performance federated search applications providing access to a list of relevant, de-duplicated information is still some way in the future.

10. Developments in Information Retrieval

A very important factor in shaping the future direction of enterprise search is research from the information retrieval community. Although there are many academic institutions undertaking information retrieval research there are also very active research groups in Google, HP, IBM, Microsoft and Oracle. There are many conferences on information retrieval, including those organized by the Special Interest Group for Information Retrieval (known as SIG IR) of the Association of Computing Machinery. Of particular importance in developing solutions to enterprise search problems are the annual TREC conferences.

The Text REtrieval Conference (TREC), co-sponsored by the National Institute of Standards and Technology (NIST) and U.S. Department of Defense, was started in 1992. Its purpose was to support research within the information retrieval community by providing the infrastructure necessary for large-scale evaluation of text retrieval methodologies. The TREC workshop series has the following goals:

- To encourage research in information retrieval based on large test collections
- To increase communication among industry, academia, and government by creating an open forum for the exchange of research ideas
- To speed the transfer of technology from research labs into commercial products by demonstrating substantial improvements in retrieval methodologies on real-world problems

- To increase the availability of appropriate evaluation techniques for use by industry and academia, including development of new evaluation techniques more applicable to current systems

Each TREC conference consists of a set of Tracks, each of which focuses in on a particular information retrieval problem, and the results are made publicly available. In the case of enterprise search, which from time to time has been a track at TREC, one of the fundamental problems is building a test collection that is representative of enterprises. Various surrogates have been used, such as a section of a public web site, but that is not going to emulate the complexity, homogeneity and scale of enterprise repositories or the requirements associated with federated searches across multiple applications.

Being able to gain access to enterprise repositories has been a major challenge for the information retrieval community because companies are concerned about the inadvertent release of confidential information in the published results from the research. In this respect the major IT companies are in a better position as they are able to use their own corporate repositories, but then have no way of knowing if the results of the research are being biased in any way.

Over the last ten years there have been a number of important meetings at which information retrieval research teams have tried to identify and prioritise areas for future research. The most recent of these (SWIRL2012) took place in Australia in early 2012 and in the preamble to the results of the workshop the observation was made:

> Throughout the decade covered by those reports, the field of Information Retrieval has continued to change and grow: collections have become larger, computers have become more powerful, broadband and mobile internet is widely assumed, complex interactive search can be done on home computers or mobile devices, and so on. Furthermore, as large-scale commercial search companies find new ways to exploit the user data they collect, the gap between the types of research done in industry and academics has widened, leading to tension about "repeatability" and "public data" in publications. These changes in environment and shifts in attitude mean the time is ripe for the field to re-evaluate its assumptions, its purposes, its goals, and its methodologies.

The themes that emerged from this workshop were:

- Not just a ranked list. This theme incorporates topics that move beyond the classic "single ad-hoc query and ranked list" approach, considering richer modes of querying, models of interaction, and approaches to answering.
- Help for users. This theme brings together topics reflecting ways that Information Retrieval technology can be extended to support users more broadly, including ways to bring IR to inexperienced, illiterate, and disabled users.

- Capturing context. This theme touches topics that look at ways to incorporate what is happening with and around a user to affect querying and result presentation. In particular, this theme treats people using search systems, their context, and their information needs as critical aspects needing exploration.

- Information, not documents. This theme crosses topics that seek to push Information Retrieval research beyond document retrieval and into more complex types of data and more complicated results.

- Domains. This theme is part of topics that consider information that is not simply text and that has not been thoroughly explored by information retrieval research so far – data with restricted access, collections of "apps," and richly connected workplace data.

- Evaluation. A perennial issue in Information Retrieval, evaluation remains important, particularly as the field expands into new challenges. This theme includes topics that require or suggest new techniques for evaluation as well as those that need evaluation in the context of new challenges.

Inevitably there is a lag between information retrieval research outcomes and their inclusion in commercial and open-source systems. The point of this section on information retrieval is that there is a substantial amount of research taking place, and increasingly this research will focus on enterprise search opportunities and challenges. A question to ask search vendors and search developers is the extent to which they are aware of this research and are ready and able to incorporate this research into their applications.

Do ask these questions the search support team needs to be monitoring developments in information retrieval as well as enterprise search technology. A good place to start is to subscribe to the Digital Library of the Association for Computing Machinery which covers a very wide range of conferences, reports and journal articles on information retrieval and enterprise search, including the conference proceedings of the ACM Special Interest Group in Information Retrieval (SIGIR).

11. Enterprise Search Professionals

Although there is a significant amount of research taking place into enterprise search there is an almost total lack of academic courses on information retrieval, let along enterprise search. There are perhaps 200 universities teaching information science and informatics at undergraduate level but information retrieval is usually only one small element of the three-year course. There are many more universities teaching computer science but again the amount of time allocated to information retrieval is very limited. The issue for companies seeking to recruit search professionals is quite bleak, and is likely to stay that way for some time to come.

One bright spot is the Lucid University, set up by LucidWorks, which offers training courses in Solr and Hadoop. However these courses are intended for developers. The company indicates that system administrators are welcome to attend, but it is primarily designed for people who have experience developing web applications in Java, PHP, Ruby or similar languages.

12. The Digital Workplace

The concept of the digital workplace is usually attributed to Jeffery Bier, who founded Instinctive Technologies in 1996. This company capitalized on the work that Bier had done at Lotus Corporation on collaborative applications, and in 2000 was re-launched as eRoom Technologies. A component of the branding was the concept of a digital workplace. Bier set out five criteria for a digital workplace which still hold good today:

- It must be comprehensible and have minimal learning curve. If people have to learn a new tool, they will not use it, especially those people outside the firewall. The digital workplace needs to be as simple and obvious as e-mail or instant messaging.

- It has to be contagious. The digital workplace must have clear benefits to all parties involved, to both distributed workers and the different enterprises interacting in these new workplaces. The workplace also has to be a trusted place, thus secure, both for the individual and the companies involved. People have to want to use it.

- It must be cross-enterprise. The digital workplace must span company boundaries and geographic boundaries. It also must operate outside the corporate firewall with an organization's customers, suppliers and other partners, and require very little IT involvement, or it will not gain acceptance.

- The workplace has to be complete. All communication, document-sharing, issues-tracking, and decision-making needs to be captured and stored in one place.

- The digital workplace must be connected. If not, it will not gain acceptance.

Of great importance in understanding the value and challenges of digital workplaces is the rise (in 1997) and disappearance (by 2005) of Enterprise Information Portals. Merrill Lynch published a seminal report on the market in November 1998 which stated:

> We believe the power of the Enterprise Portal lies in the fact that from a single gateway, users will be able to find, extract and analyze all of this information. Furthermore, we also believe that these new EIP systems will shift the focus away from the actual content of the information to the context in which the end user consumes the information, whether the end user is an employee, customer or supplier. In this way information consumers will finally be able to benefit from data and information by accessing, mining and transferring it into disparate applications where it can be used again.

The vision was ahead not only of the technology but also of organizations realizing that they were not managing information effectively. This is now changing slowly and is beginning to open up an achievable vision of a digital workplace where search will be a very important enabling technology not just as a means of finding information but of integrating a wide range of applications.

13. Does 'enterprise search' Have a Future?

There is an on-going debate about what the term 'enterprise search' means and whether there is a better description. In the planning stages of this book there was a discussion about whether 'Enterprise Search' was the best title, but none of the team behind this book could come up with a better title. I might argue that the concept is one of business intelligence but that term has already been taken, though arguably it has nothing to do with intelligence!

In the final analysis enterprise search is vision and not one or more pieces of software. All employees should have effective access to the information that the organization has created and collected so that they can make well-informed decisions that benefit the organization and their own careers. It is inconceivable that a manufacturer would invest in a precision machine tool, put it in a shed on the factory site and not tell anyone of its existence. And yet every day that is the fate of digital information assets.

At long last organizations are recognizing the strategic and operational value of information and taking action. The biggest single barrier to effective implementation is finding people with the skills needed to understand how to get the best out of the sophisticated technology of search so that the technology does not stand between a query and an index but links them intuitively.

Without these people we may end up echoing the words of T.S Elliott in the Opening Stanza from Choruses from "The Rock":

"Where is the wisdom we have lost in knowledge?

Where is the knowledge we have lost in information?"

Further Reading

You'll find some additional information regarding the subject matter of this chapter in the "Further Reading" (page 156) section in Appendix A.

CHAPTER 12

Critical Success Factors

After eleven chapters and over 60,000 words I thought you might find it useful to have a short list of 12 critical success factors.

1. Invest in a search support team

Before you do anything else set up a search support team with the skills, enthusiasm, organizational knowledge and networks to get the best of the current search application(s). Even if the team is initially a team of one put the budget, headcount and job descriptions in place so that it can grow ahead of the requirements for support.

2. Get the best out of the current investment in search

There is usually much that can be done to improve the current search applications once the search team and the search vendor focus in on options and priorities. The information gained from search log files is a very important element of defining search requirements and setting benchmarks for any new search application

3. Enterprise search is an approach and not a technology

Implementing one single all-encompassing search application is unlikely to be successful and usually carries more risks than benefits. Enterprise search is about creating a managed search environment that ensures employees find the information they need to achieve organizational and/or personal objectives.

4. Set search within an information management context

If the organization does not see information as a business asset it will never invest enough into search and is very susceptible to competitive and reputation risks. An information management strategy owned by a senior manager is an essential prerequisite to successful search.

5. Content quality is essential for quality search

Good search technology will quickly reveal poor content. There should be guidelines for content and metadata quality. It is of little benefit to the organization if a search lists twenty relevant documents with a content quality that renders them unfit to be trusted.

6. Understand user requirements and monitor user satisfaction

Relevance is a personal measure of information value. Basing a business case on anecdotal information about the current search application and what other organizations have achieved with a particular piece of technology is not a suitable basis for an investment decision. It could be your career prospects that suffer.

7. Search then browse then alert then search then alert....

Users need to be able to search when needed, browse when needed and set up alerts as needed. These three processes need to be linked together to provide an effective information discovery environment.

8. Provide location-independent search

The search application should be as effective via remote access desktops, smartphones and tablets as it is on a large screen monitor in the IT department. Not all search vendors have recognized the need for innovation in user interfaces for mobile devices.

9. Undertake intelligent log analysis

Search log analysis needs to be conducted on a regular basis by a team that understands the activities and language of the business so that emerging issues in search failure can be identified at the earliest possible opportunity

10. Search is a dialogue

Aiming to get the most relevant documents at the top of the first page of results is a waste of effort. In an enterprise environment users will have complex queries that require them to be able to refine their query and re-evaluate the results with the minimum of effort.

11. Procure value not functionality

When the time comes to invest in a new search application specify requirements in terms of what your users expect the search application to deliver and not on what features you would like to have supplied.

12. Search is a journey

The process of ensuring that search is meeting user requirements never comes to an end. Every day there are new employees, new business challenges, new business opportunities, and new developments in search technology. Search should never be a 'project' but instead be a way of working.

Resources

Enterprise Search – A Reading List

This is a list of some of the books published since 2006 on enterprise search, information retrieval, and text mining.

Ambient Findability, Peter Morville (2005). O'Reilly Publishing.

The Answer Machine, Susan Feldman (2012). Morgan and Claypool Publishers.

Apache Solr 3.1 Cookbook, Rafa Ku (2011). PACKT Publishing.

Book of Search, (Out of print) Kjetil Halvorsen et al., (2006). Fast Search and Transfer.

Designing Search: UX Strategies for eCommerce Success, Greg Nudelman (2011). Wiley Publishing.

Designing the Search Experience, Tony Russell-Rose and Tyler Tate (2013). Morgan Kaufmann Publishers.

Economic Trends in Enterprise Search Solutions, Pierre-Jean Benghozi and Cécile Chamaret (2010). Institute for Prospective Technological Studies, Joint Research Centre, European Commission.

Enterprise Search in Action, Mark Teutelink (2011). Manning Publications Company.

Enterprise Search and Retrieval, 2011/2012. Ovum.

Enterprise Search Vendor Evaluations, Version 4.0. (2011). The Real Story Group.

Faceted Search, Daniel Tunkelang (2010). Morgan and Claypool Publishers.

Feature Centric View of Information Retrieval, Donald Metzler (2011). Springer.

Foundations of Large-Scale Multimedia Information Management and Retrieval, Edward Y. Chang (2011). Springer.

Fundamentals of Predictive Text Mining, Sholom M. Weiss, Nitin Indurkhya, and Tong Zhang (2010). Springer.

Google's PageRank and Beyond: The Science of Search Engine Rankings, Amy N. Langville and Carl D. Mayer (2006). Princeton University Press.

Information Retrieval: Algorithms and Heuristics, 2nd Edition, David A. Grossman and Ophir Frieder (2004). Springer.

Information Retrieval Evaluation, Donna Harman (2011). Morgan and Claypool Publishers.

Information Retrieval: Implementing and Evaluating Search Engines, Stefan Büttcher, Charles L. A. Clarke, and Gordon V. Cormack (2010). Massachusetts Institute of Technology.

Information Retrieval: Searching in the 21st Century, Ayse Goker and John Davies (Editors) (2009). Wiley-Blackwell.

Innovations in Information Retrieval: Perspectives for theory and practice, Allen Foster and Pauline Rafferty (Editors) (2011). Facet Publishing.

Interactive Information Seeking, Behaviour and Retrieval, Ian Ruthven and Diane Kelly (Editors) (2011). Facet Publishing.

Introduction to Information Retrieval, Christopher D. Manning, Prabhakar Raghavan, and Hinrich Schutze (2008). Cambridge University Press.

Introduction to Modern Information Retrieval, G. G. Chowdhury (2010). Facet Publishing.

Lucene in Action, Michael McCandless, Erik Hatcher, and Otis Gospodnetic (2010). Manning Publications.

Making Search Work, Martin White (2007). Facet Publishing.

Multilingual Information Retrieval: From Research To Practice. Carol Peters, Martin Braschler, and Paul Clough (2011). Springer.

Multimedia Information Retrieval, Stefan Rüger (2009). Morgan and Claypool Publishers.

Modern Information Retrieval: The Concepts and Technology Behind Search, Ricardo Baeza-Yates and Berthier Ribeiro-Neto. 2nd Edition. (2011). Addison Wesley.

New Landscape of Enterprise Search, Stephen Arnold (2011). Pandia Search Central.

Professional Microsoft Search, Mark Bennett, Jeff Fried, Miles Kehoe, and Natalya Voskresenskaya (2011). Wrox.

Prospects of Mobile Search, Jose Luis Gomez-Barroso et al., (2010). Institute for Prospective Technological Studies, Joint Research Centre, European Commission.

Search Analytics For Your Site, Louis Rosenfeld (2011). Rosenfeld Media.

Search-Based Applications: At the Confluence of Search and Database Technologies, Gregory Grefenstette and Laura Wilber (2010). Morgan and Claypool Publishers.

Search Engines: Information Retrieval in Practice, W. Bruce Croft, Donald Metzler, and Trevor Strohman (2010). Addison Wesley.

Search Patterns, Peter Morville and Jefferey Callender (2010). O'Reilly Publishing.

Search User Interfaces, Marti A. Hearst (2009). Cambridge University Press.

Search User Interfaces Design, Max Wilson (2012). Morgan and Claypool Publishers.

Semantic Software Technologies, Lynda Moulton (2010). Gilbane Group.

Successful Enterprise Search Management, Stephen Arnold and Martin White. 2010. Galatea Publishing.

Teaching and Learning in Information Retrieval, E. Efthimiadis, J.M.Fernández-Lunam J.F.Huete and A. MacFarlane. 2011. Springer.

Text Mining: Advanced Approaches in Analyzing Unstructured Data, Ronen Feldman and James Sanger (2006). Cambridge University Press.

Text Mining: Applications and Theory, Michael W. Berry and Jacob Kogan (Editors) (2010). Wiley-Blackwell.

Understanding Information Retrieval Systems: Management, Types, and Standards, Marica J. Bates (Editor) (2011). Auerbach Publications.

Working with Microsoft FAST Search Server 2010 for SharePoint, Mikael Svenson, Marcus Johansson, and Robert Piddocke (2012) Microsoft Press.

Enterprise Search - Blogs

This page is a list of blogs which track developments in enterprise search technology and implementation. Some of these blogs are published by search vendors. Others (such as the Real Story Group blog) cover a range of topics including enterprise search. This list was checked in September 2012.

Attensity Blog (*http://blog.attensity.com/*)

Basis Technology (*http://info.basistech.com/blog*)

Beyond Search (Stephen Arnold) (*http://arnoldit.com/wordpress/*)

Concept Searching (*http://www.conceptsearching.com/wp/category/smartcontentdiscussions/*)

Coveo Insights (*http://blog.coveo.com/*)

Darwin Awareness Engine (*http://www.darwineco.com/blog/*)

Do More With Search (BA Insight) (*http://www.domorewithsearch.com/*)

Enterprise Search (New Idea Engineering) (*http://www.enterprisesearchblog.com/*)

Enterprise Search (Lynda Moulton) (*http://bluebillinc.com/author/lynda-moulton/*)

Exalead (*http://blog.exalead.com/*)

Flax (*http://www.flax.co.uk/blog/*)

Findability (Findwise) (*http://www.findwise.com/blog/*)

Google Enterprise (*http://googleenterprise.blogspot.co.uk/*)

Information Interaction (Tony Russell-Rose) (*http://isquared.wordpress.com/*)

Information Optimized (Vivisimo - discontinued from 09/2012 but the archive remains live) (*http://informationoptimized.com/*)

Mindbreeze (*http://blog.mindbreeze.com/*)

Noisy Channel (Daniel Tunkelang) (*http://thenoisychannel.com/*)

Perfect Search (*http://www.perfectsearchcorp.com/Blog.aspx*)

Polyspot Blog (*http://www.polyspot.com/en/blog/*)

Real Story Group Blog (*http://www.realstorygroup.com/Blog/*)

Searchblox (*http://www.searchblox.com/blog-2*)

Search Chronicles (Paul Nelson, Search Technologies) (*http://www.searchtechnologies.com/searchchronicles.html*)

Search Hub Lucid Works (*http://searchhub.org/dev/*)

Sematext Blog (*http://blog.sematext.com/*)

Sinequa's Blog (*http://blog.sinequa.com/*)

SmartLogic Journal (*http://www.smartlogic.com/home/news-and-events/journal*)

The Core Perspective Recommind (*http://blog.recommind.com/*)

Unified Information Access (Attivio) (*http://www.attivio.com/blog.html*)

There is also a very good LinkedIn Enterprise Search Engine Professionals Group. Membership is by application.

Further Reading

Here you'll find a list of further readings recommended for the following chapters.

Chapter 1 Readings

Unlocking the Value of the Information Economy (http://eval.symantec.com/mktginfo/ enterprise/other_resources/bhbr_unlocking_value_info_economy_21028773.en-us.pdf), (2011). Harvard Business Review Analytic Services.

"The Post-Relational Reality Sets In" (*http://www.marklogic.com/news-and-events/press-releases/2011/marklogic-survey-reveals-unstructured-information-is-growing-rapidly-will-soon-surpass-relational-data/*) , (2011). Survey on Unstructured Data. MarkLogic.

Mind the Enterprise Search Gap (*http://www.smartlogic.com/home/news-and-events/press-releases/1657-mind-the-enterprise-search-gap-smartlogic-sponsor-mindmetre-research-report*), (2011). SmartLogic.

"Enterprise Search and Findability Survey" (*http://news.findwise.com/pressrelease/view/no-strategy-no-budget-no-resources-yet-enterprise-search-is-considered-critical-success-factor-in-75-of-organisations-responding-to-global-777161*), (2012). Findwise.

From Overload to Impact: An Industry Scorecard to Big Data Business Challenges (*http://www.oracle.com/us/industries/industry-scorecard-1683398.html*) , (2012). Oracle.

Chapter 2 Readings

The Name Matching You Need (*http://www.basistech.com/whitepapers/*), (2011). Basis Technologies.

Chapter 3 Readings

Rosenfeld Media (*http://rosenfeldmedia.com/*) specializes in books on determining user requirements and the development of user interfaces.

The User is Always Right, Steve Mulder with Ziv Yaar (2007). New Riders Publishing.

Ad-hoc Personas and Empathetic Focus (*http://www.jnd.org/dn.mss/adhoc_personas_em.html*), Donald Norman.

Chapter 4 Readings

"Enterprise Search and Findability Survey" (*http://news.findwise.com/pressrelease/view/no-strategy-no-budget-no-resources-yet-enterprise-search-is-considered-critical-success-factor-in-75-of-organisations-responding-to-global-777161*), (2012). Findwise.

Digital Workplace Trends (*http://www.digital-workplace-trends.com/*), NetStrategy/JMC.

Chapter 6 Readings

The Name Matching You Need (*http://www.basistech.com/whitepapers/*), (2011). Basis Technologies.

The Answer Machine, Susan Feldman (2012). Morgan and Claypool Publishers (*http://www.morganclaypool.com*).

Chapter 7 Readings

New Landscape of Enterprise Search (http://www.pandia.com/enterprise-search/), Stephen Arnold (2011). Pandia Search Central.

Enterprise Search (http://www.realstorygroup.com/Research/Search/), Real Story Group.

Beyond Search – News and Information About Search and Content Processing (http://arnoldit.com/wordpress/)

Chapter 8 Readings

Enterprise Search (http://www.realstorygroup.com/Research/Search/), Real Story Group.

Chapter 9 Readings

Professional Microsoft Search, Mark Bennett, Jeff Fried, Miles Kehoe, and Natalya Vosrensenskaya (2010). Wrox (*http://www.wrox.com/WileyCDA/*).

Working With Microsoft FAST Search Server 2010 for SharePoint. Mikael Svenson, Marcus Johansson, and Robert Piddocke (2012). Microsoft Press (*http://www.microsoft.com/learning/en/us/training/format-books.aspx*).

Although these two books are specifically about SharePoint search implementation they both illustrate the work involved in installation and implementation.

Chapter 10 Readings

Search Analytics for Your Site, Louis Rosenfeld (2010). Rosenfeld Media (*http://rosenfeldmedia.com/*).

Chapter 11 Readings

The Answer Machine, Susan Feldman (2012). Morgan and Claypool Publishers (*http://www.morganclaypool.com*).

Search-Based Applications. , Gregory Grefenstette and Laura Wilber (2011). Morgan and Claypool Publishers.

Reshaping the Workforce With the New Analytics, Technology Forecast (2012). PwC (*http://www.pwc.com/us/en/technology-forecast/index.jhtml*).

Semantic Software Technologies - Landscape of High Value Added Applications for the Enterprise, Lynda Moulton (2010). Gilbane Group.

Second Strategic Workshop on Information Retrieval in Lorne, (2012). *http://www.cs.rmit.edu.au/swirl12/*.

Vendor List

This table lists over 70 vendors. Not all are search software vendors. Also included are vendors providing a range of ancillary services and some of the many vendors providing data analysis and business intelligence software. In the case of major corporations only the home page URL has been provided as the pages for search products tend to be far from permanent. All links were verified in September 2012. No warranty is given by Intranet Focus Ltd or the author.

Company	Country	URL
Active Navigation	UK	http://www.activenav.com/
Alcove9	USA	http://www.alcove9.com
Amazon	USA	http://a9.com/
Ankiro	Denmark	http://www.ankiro.com
Apache (Lucene/Solr)	Community	http://lucene.apache.org
Applied Relevance	USA	http://www.appliedrelevance.com
Attensity	USA	http://www.attensity.com
Attivio	USA	http://www.attivio.com
Autonomy (HP)	UK	http://www.autonomy.com
BA-Insight	USA	http://www.bainsight.com
Basis	USA	http://www.basistech.com
Brainware	USA	http://www.perceptivesoftware.com
Clearwell	USA	http://www.clearwellsystems.com/
Cognition Systems	USA	http://cognition.com
Commvault	USA	http://www.comvault.com
Concept Searching	UK	http://www.conceptsearching.com
Constellio	Canada	http://www.constellio.com

Company	Country	URL
Coveo	Canada	http://www.conveo.com
Dieselpoint	USA	http://www.dieselpoint.com
Digital Reasoning	USA	http://digitalreasoning.com
dtSearch	USA	http://www.dtsearch.com
EMC	USA	http://www.emc.com
ElasticSearch	Netherlands	http://www.elasticsearch.com
Endeca	USA	http://www.oracle.com
Exalead	France	http://www.3ds.com/products/exalead
Exorbyte	USA	http://www.exorbyte.com
Expert System	Italy	http://www.expertsystem.net
Fabasoft	Austria	http://www.mindbreeze.com/en
Funnelback	Australia	http://www.funnelback.com
Google	USA	http://www.google.com/enterprise/search/products_gsa.html
IBM	USA	http://www.ibm.com
Inbenta	Spain	http://www.inbenta.com
Infosys	USA	http://www.infosys.com
InQuira	USA	http://www.oracle.com
Intelligenx	USA	http://www.intelligenx.com
Intrafind	Germany	http://www.intrafind.de
ISYS	Australia	www.perceptivesoftware.com
Karmasphere	USA	http://www.karmasphere.com
Lexalytics	USA	http://www.lexalytics.com
LTU	France	http://www.ltutech.com
Lucid Works	USA	http://www.lucidworks.com
Mark Logic	USA	http://www.marklogic.com
MaxxCAT	USA	http://www.maxxcat.com
Microsoft	USA	http://www.microsoft.com
Omniture	USA	http://www.omniture.com
OpenSearchServer	France	http://www.open-search-server.com
OpenText	Canada	http://www.opentext.com
Oracle	USA	http://www.oracle.com
Perfect Search	USA	http://www.perfectsearchcorp.com
Polyspot	France	http://www.polyspot.com
Q-Sensei	USA	http://www.qsensei.com/
Recommind	USA	http://www.recommind.com
SAP	Germany	http://www.sap.com

Company	Country	URL
SchemaLogic	USA	http://www.schemalogic.com
SearchBlox	USA	http://www.searchblox.com
SearchDaimon	Sweden	http://www.searchdaimon.com
Sematext	USA	http://sematext.com
Sinequa	France	http://www.sinequa.com
Smart Logic	UK	http://www.smartlogic.com
Sophia Systems	UK	http://www.sophiasearch.com
Sphinx	Community	http://sphinxsearch.com
Stored IQ	USA	http://www.storediq.com
SurfRay	Denmark	http://www.surfray.com
Synaptica	USA	http://www.synaptica.com
Temis	France	http://temis.com
Teragram	USA	http://www.teragram.com/oem
TeraText	USA	http://www.teratext.com
Terrier	UK	http://terrier.org
Thetus	USA	http://thetus.com
Thunderstone	USA	http://www.thunderstone.com
Vivisimo	USA	http://www.vivisimo.com
Wand	USA	http://wandinc.com
Xapian	Community	http://xapian.org
X1 Technologies	USA	http://www.x1.com
ZyLab	USA	http://zylab.com

Search integration specialists.

All links were verified in September 2012. No warranty is given by Intranet Focus Ltd or the author.

Capax Global	USA	http://www.capaxglobal.com
Comperio	Norway	http://www.comperiosearch.com
Enterprise Data Fusion	USA	http://www.edatafusion.com/
Findwise	Sweden	http://www.findwise.com
Flax	UK	http://www.flax.co.uk
New Idea Engineering	USA	http://www.ideaeng.com
Raytion	Germany	http://www.raytion.com
Search Technologies	USA	http://www.searchtechnologies.com
Tieto	Finland	http://www.tieto.com
TNR Global	USA	http://tnrsearch.com

Glossary

Adjacent result

A result that is comparable or analogous to a searched term; often produced by "Find more like this" searches.

Absolute boosting

Ensuring that a specified document always appears at the same point in a results set, or always appears on the first page of results

Access Control List (ACL)

Defines permissions to access a specific repository, a set of documents or a section of a document

Ambiguity

A search involving one word with many different meanings, or in a search for an object that can be described many different ways.

Appliance

A search application pre-installed on a server ready for insertion into a standard server rack

Approximate Pattern Matching

A process in which an algorithm determines the similarity between items, for example in spell checking

Automatic Indexing

An entirely automated process of converting information into an index

Auto-categorization

An automated process for creating a classification system (or taxonomy) from a collection of nominally related documents.

Auto-classification

An automated process for assigning metadata or index values to documents, usually in conjunction with an existing taxonomy.

Average response time

An average of the time taken for the search engine to respond to a query, or the average end-to-end time of a query.

Bayesian Inference or Bayesian Statistics

A probability technique based on the work of Thomas Bayes (1702-1761) and used to determine the relevancy of a given document against a particular query.

BigTable

A highly scalable database technology that is proprietary to Google.

Boolean Operators

A widely used approach to create search queries. Examples include and, or, and not, e.g., John and Smith.

Boolean Search

A search query using Boolean operators.

Boosting

The changing of a parameter of a search to ensure that a certain object or objects appear in the results.

Case-Based Reasoning

A technology that allows a system to "learn" by gathering past instances into a "case base" that it can use to solve future problems.

Categorization

The placing of boundaries around objects that share similarities, e.g., taxonomy.

Clustering

A process employed to generate groupings of related words by identifying patterns in a document index.

Collection

A group of objects methodically sorted and placed into a category.

Computational linguistics

The use of computer-based statistical analysis of language to determine patterns and rules that aid semantic understanding

Concept extraction

The process of determining concepts from text using linguistic analysis

Connector

A software application that enables a search application to index content in another application

Controlled Vocabulary

An organized list of words, phrases, or some other set employed to identify and retrieve documents.

Corpus

A collection of objects with a defined scope. E.g. all annual reports

COTS

Commercial-Of-The-Shelf software

Crawler

A program used to index documents.

See Also Spider.

Description

A brief statement in a document that effectively summarizes the meaning of a document, often employed to annotate search results.

See Also Key Sentence.

Document

A structured sequence of text information, but often used as a generic description of any content item in a search application

Document processing

The de-construction of a document into a form that can be tokenised and indexed

Document Repository

A site where source documents or other content objects are stored, generally a folder or folders.

See Also Information Source.

Early binding

A search is conducted only across documents that a user has permission to access.

See Also Late binding.

Entity extraction

The automatic detection of defined items in a document, such as dates, times, locations, names and acronymns

Exact Match

Two or more words considered mutually inclusive in a search, often by enclosing them in quotation marks, e.g., "United Nations."

Extract-Transform-Load

The process of migrating content between databases when undertaken by a single specialised software application

Facet

Presentation of topic categories on the search user interface to support the refinement of a search query.

Fallout

A quantity representing the percentage of irrelevant hits retrieved in a search.

Federated search

A search carried out across multiple repositories and/or applications.

Field Query

A search that is limited to a specific field in a document, e.g. a title or date.

Filter

A function that sets specific criteria for search results.

Free Text Query

A search enabling a user to input words in any form, without following any query language criteria.

Freshness

The time period between a document being crawled and the index being updated so that a user will be able to find the document.

Fuzzy Search

A search allowing a degree of flexibility for generating hits, i.e., matches that are phonetically or typographically similar.

Golden Set

A set of documents and other content that is representative of content that will be searched on a regular basis that can be used to benchmark search performance.

Guided Search

A search in which the system prompts the user for information that will refine the search results.

Hit

A search result matching given criteria.

Index

List containing data and/or metadata indicating the identity and location of a given file or document.

Index File

A file that stores data in a format capable of retrieval by a search engine.

Indexer (automatic)

A program that collects data on a given set of files or documents and provides results for a user search.

Indexer (human)

A person who assigns metadata to a given set of files or documents and makes results available for a user search.

Information Source

The location of indexed documents.

See Also Document Repository.

Ingestion Rate

The rate at which documents can be indexed, usually specified in Mb/sec

Inverse Document Frequency (IDF)

A measure of the rarity of a given term in a file or document collection.

Inverted File

A list of the words contained within a set of documents, and which document each word is present in.

Inverted Index

An index whose entries identify a given word and the documents in which it appears.

Iterative Calculation

A calculation utilizing a recursive and self-referential algorithm.

Key Sentence

A brief statement that effectively summarizes a document, often employed to annotate search results. .

Keyword

A word used in a query to search for documents.

Keyword Search

A search that compares an inputted word against an index and returns matching results.

Keyword Targeting

A process which helps to ensure the inclusion of given web sites in a search for a specific object.

Knowledge Extraction

The procurement of metadata from a given set of objects.

Late binding

A search carried out across a complete repository of documents when a check is carried out on access permissions immediately before the presentation of the document to the user.

See Also Early binding.

Lemmatization

A process that identifies root form of a words contained within a given document based on grammatical analysis (e.g., run from running).

See Also Stemming.

Lexical Analysis

An analysis that reduces a text to a set of discrete words, sentences and paragraphs.

Linguistics

The study of the structure, use and development of language

Linguistic Indexing

The classification of a set of words into grammatical classes, such as noun or verb.

Meta Search Engine

A class of search engine that generally retrieves information to user queries by utilizing other search engines.

Meta Tag

An HTML command located within the header of a website that displays additional or referential data not present on the page itself.

Metadata

Metadata is data about data,

Morphologic analysis

The analysis of the structure of language

Natural Language Processing

A process that identifies content by attempting to adhere to the rules of a given language.

Natural Language Query

A search input entered using conventional language, e.g., a sentence.

Parametric Search

A search that adheres to predefined attributes present within a given data source.

Parsing

The process of analysing text to determine its semantic structure

Pattern Matching

Pattern matching recognizes naturally occurring patterns (word usage, frequency of use, etc.) within a document.

Phrase Extraction

The procurement of linguistic concepts, generally phrases, from a given document.

Precision

The quantification of the number of correct documents returned in a given search.

Probabilistic Method

A method that utilizes user-supplied information to determine the probability that a given word appears in a document.

Proximity Searching

A search whose results are returned based on the proximity of given words.

Query by Example

A search in which a previously returned result is used to obtain similar results.

Query Performance

A measure of performance based on the speed a system can receive a query and return results.

Query transformation

The process of analyzing the semantic structure of a query prior to processing in order to improve search performance

Ranking

A value assigned to a specific result returned for a query. The first item listed has a ranking of 1, the second has a ranking of 2, etc.

Recall

A percentage representing the relationship between correct results generated by a query and the total number of correct results within an index.

Relevance

The value that a user places on a specific document or item of information.

Relevance Ranking

See Ranking.

Search Results

The documents or data that are returned from a search.

Search Terms

The terms used within a search field.

Semantic Analysis

An analysis based upon grammatical or syntactical constraints that attempts to decipher information contained in a document.

Sentiment analysis

The use of of natural language processing, computational linguistics, and text analytics to identify and extract subjective information in documents

Soundex Search

A search in which the user receives results that are phonetically similar to their query.

Spider

An automated process that provides documents to a data extraction or parsing engine.

See Also Crawler.

Statistical Indexing

Probabilistic methods relying on mathematics, not "linguistics." See Bayesian.

Stemming

A process based on a set of heuristic rules that identifies the root form of words contained within a given document (e.g., run from running).

See Also Lemmatization.

Stop words

Words that are deemed to have no value in an index

Structured Data

Data that can be represented according to specific descriptive parameters, e.g., rows and columns in a relational database, or hierarchical nodes in an XML document or fragment.

Summarization

An automated process for producing a short summary of a document and presenting it in the list of results

Synonym expansion

Automatically expanding a search by adding synonymns of the query terms derived from a thesaurus.

Syntactic Analysis

An analysis capable of associating a word with its respective part of speech by determining its context in a given statement.

Taxonomy

In respect to search, the broad categorization of objects (typically a tree structure of classifications for a given set of objects) in order to make them easier to retrieve and possibly sort.

Term Frequency

A quantity representing how often a term appears in a document.

Thesaurus

A collection of words in a cross-reference system that refers to multiple taxonomies and provides a kind of meta-classification, thereby facilitating document retrieval.

TREC

Text Retrieval Conference, a conference held by the National Institute of Standards and Technology in which participants search a collection of documents and present results on various search metrics.

Tokenising

The process of identifying the elements of a sentence, such as phrases, words, abbreviations and symbols, prior to the creation of an index.

Truncation

The removal from a prefix of suffix.

Unstructured Information

Information that is without document or data structure (i.e., cannot be effectively decomposed into constituent elements or chunks for atomic storage and management).

Vector space

A model that enables documents to be ranked for relevance against a query by comparing an algebraic expression of a set of documents with that of the query.

Weight

A value applied to a given area of a search system, e.g., term weighting, which represents its importance with respect to other factors.

Wildcard

A notation, generally an asterisk or question mark which, when used in a query, represents all possible characters, e.g., a search for boo* would return book, boom, boot, etc.

Word Exclusion and Stop Lists

A list containing words that will not be indexed, usually words that are excessively common, e.g., a, an, the, etc.

Word Proximity Analysis

An analysis that measures the distance between searched words in a document.

About the Author

Martin White is an information management consultant specialising in enterprise search assignments. He established Intranet Focus Ltd in 1999 and has been a Visiting Professor at the iSchool, University of Sheffield since 2002. He is a Fellow of the Royal Society of Chemistry and a Member of the Association of Computing Machinery.

Have it your way.

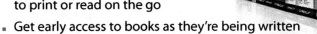

Get even more for your money.

Join the O'Reilly Community, and register the O'Reilly books you own. It's free, and you'll get:

- $4.99 ebook upgrade offer
- 40% upgrade offer on O'Reilly print books
- Membership discounts on books and events
- Free lifetime updates to ebooks and videos
- Multiple ebook formats, DRM FREE
- Participation in the O'Reilly community
- Newsletters
- Account management
- 100% Satisfaction Guarantee

Signing up is easy:

1. **Go to: oreilly.com/go/register**
2. **Create an O'Reilly login.**
3. **Provide your address.**
4. **Register your books.**

Note: English-language books only

To order books online:
oreilly.com/store

For questions about products or an order:
orders@oreilly.com

To sign up to get topic-specific email announcements and/or news about upcoming books, conferences, special offers, and new technologies:
elists@oreilly.com

For technical questions about book content:
booktech@oreilly.com

To submit new book proposals to our editors:
proposals@oreilly.com

O'Reilly books are available in multiple DRM-free ebook formats. For more information:
oreilly.com/ebooks

O'REILLY®

Spreading the knowledge of innovators   oreilly.com

CPSIA information can be obtained at www.ICGtesting.com
Printed in the USA
BVOW01s1535221014

371912BV00021B/495/P